DRAMA

IN THE CLASSROOM

CREATIVE ACTIVITIES
FOR TEACHERS, PARENTS & FRIENDS

POLLY ERION

Lost Coast Press
Fort Bragg, California

For more information, or to order additional copies, contact the publisher:

Lost Coast Press
155 Cypress Street
Fort Bragg CA 95437
1-800-773-7782
www.cypresshouse.com

Library of Congress Cataloging-in-Publication Data

Erion, Polly.
　　　Drama in the classroom : creative activities for teachers, parents, and friends / by Polly Erion.
　　　　　p.cm.
　　　Includes bibliographical references and index.
　　　ISBN 1-882897-04-8
　　　1. Drama in education.　2. Play.　3. Early childhood education—Activity programs.　I. Title.

PN3171.E75 1996
371.3'32—dc20　　　　　　　　　　　　　　　　96-5640
　　　　　　　　　　　　　　　　　　　　　　　　　CIP

Clip art courtesy of Corel Presentation Exchange

Book production by Cypress House

Printed by Thomson-Shore, Inc.

Manufactured in the USA

8 9 7

DEAR TEACHERS, PARENTS AND FRIENDS:

THIS BOOK has been a labor of love. At times I felt it was an impossible task, but the strong desire to share with you has led to its completion. I strongly believe that drama helps everyone gain confidence and a better sense of self. Adult and child alike are involved in both teaching and learning through the process of intuitive discovery. Drama provides an ideal media for stimulating intuition and for finding a way to relate to our common humanity.

Experience has shown me that I learn best when actively involved in a tangible or emotional way. Mental pictures, simulated experience and the use of any or all of my five senses help to internalize a concept or give a more lasting meaning. In later life I have identified myself as possibly having had several learning disabilities. Years ago we did not spend as much time studying problems, but found more practical ways to deal with them. My feeling is that too much labeling of children can be harmful. Positive and creative activities help restore confidence-and confidence is the key to any type of success. The solution to my difficulties I found largely in the arts and have therefore found the arts most useful in my teaching. Drama became the media for me to use to incorporate all of the arts with the curriculum and assist the learning process. I became the "learner" as well as the teacher and came to realize that most of these lessons help adults as well as children. Drama helps anyone focus more effectively and find that part of ourselves that is truly creative.

The activities included in this book are ones that can be used as an adjunct or even an integral part of a regular curriculum; by parents at home, working and playing with their children; and even by adults seeking more creativity in their lives.

Polly Erion

FOREWORD

OVID, THE LATIN POET, at about 20 B.C., wrote, "There is a deity within us who breathes that divine fire by which we are animated." There is a great need today for that deity to be acknowledged, and that fire rekindled so that our children may be reanimated.

Polly Erion is rekindling that fire in children with her book, Drama in the Classroom. This book, written for parents and teachers, contains the answers to many questions concerning children and their problems. It provides enough inspired material to give a classroom teacher years of help in those agonizing times of "How do I handle this?" Or "What do I do now?" Polly feels that we have not paid sufficient attention to the functions of the right hemisphere of the brain. She found, as she used drama in the classrooms where she was teaching, that children who had been classified as slow learners and behavior problems were predominantly right-brained.

As she worked with these children, encouraging them to participate in dramatic activities and perform in skits and plays, some written by the students themselves, she began to hear from their teachers and parents that these students were improving measurably in *left-brained* skills, and were causing fewer problems in the classrooms. Their self-esteem was raised, and they became more cooperative and animated in positive ways.

Polly's creativity and imagination are demonstrated in the activities which accompany and elucidate the lessons. Her various ideas are wonderful for the development of intuition. They help children recognize their use of intuition and learn to trust it. In these days, when society is giving so many mixed messages, it is important for children to learn to see what they see, feel what they feel, and know what they know.

Polly's years of working with children have earned her the recognition and love of thousands of children and teachers with whom she has been involved.

I am sure you will find your own fire rekindled as you use this book.

Laurene Jensen, Educator
Principal, Mae Carden Schools

INTRODUCTION

THIS BOOK contains a variety of ideas for the use of drama in the education of children. Not just play acting, but the kind of drama that involves the varieties of ways we learn and express ourselves. Drama can help young people find their true and unique selves; appreciate the talents and needs of others; feel the satisfaction of working successfully with a group; develop skills which will be useful for other endeavors; help add meaning to factual material; and provide a safe working atmosphere that is as free as possible from fear and competition.

Children gain confidence through dramatic activities. They can express themselves dramatically in a thousand acceptable ways. Learning to control their emotions and behavior gives them a stronger sense of self. I never cease to be amazed at the way a child with the least selfdiscipline, the wiggliest and most obstreperous, will often win at activities requiring a perfect freeze or intense concentration. These children frequently become good leaders when they redirect their energy and talents in a positive way.

It is not only important for children to discover their own attributes; but to learn to enjoy and appreciate the talents of others. Such appreciation builds character. Drama provides an opportunity for children to give support and encouragement to peers with special needs; the shy ones, those with handicaps of one type or another, and those children who have difficulty focusing or attending. Very frequently children who have been unsuccessful academically find creative talents which spark them into other areas of success.

Group work lends itself very effectively to drama. Sometimes children work in pairs, and other times groups range from three on up to include the entire class. Always, the emphasis is on being considerate so that feelings do not get hurt. Leaders emerge, but children do come to learn that to be an effective leader, one must also be willing to cooperate. I love drama for many reasons and this is one of the major ones. I see classes do a turn-around from being chaotic and negative to being motivated and supportive. I see individual children bloom with confidence and success.

Two skills which are strongly emphasized in drama are concentration and communication. Developing the ability to focus, to think of one thing only, to *concentrate*, is an invaluable skill and when applied to any learning process, greatly increases the power to acquire that skill. When focus is applied to drama, stage fright disappears and talent emerges. Communicating with one another comes naturally, but communicating with an audience effectively and comfortably usually requires much practice. Much of the emphasis in drama is on being considerate to the audience so the speakers or actors are encouraged to speak clearly and make their actions effective.

Factual material can become much more meaningful when drama enhances the curriculum. Children are encouraged to research their own material, involving their whole selves rather than just regurgitating memorized facts. Even those who learn academic material easily benefit from a more creative approach. Since fear stifles intelligence, and intelligence is necessary for real learning to take place, a safe atmosphere becomes the priority. When speaking of intelligence, I'm not referring to I.Q. but that kind of mind that retains its curiosity and ability to focus. This is possible only when a child is free of fear. This is why the one rule or goal, is simply teaching to *be considerate*. Children need to learn to trust their teachers and each other in order to feel safe. Safety builds confidence and confidence builds intelligence.

This book contains a wide variety of lessons, activities and exercises designed to achieve the following goals: individualization, creativity, successful group work, skill development, academic enhancement and, perhaps the most important of all, self confidence. These goals can only be realized in a safe but stimulating atmosphere.

The following are some questions which I thought you might have. I have tried to keep my answers brief.

What does drama include and how do I define it?

Drama includes all creative activities, conceptual learning and whole body involvement. It is not just *play acting*, as is sometimes commonly thought. Technically speaking, we have a two-hemisphere brain and drama is unique in the way it can help the analytical, rational left brain work in interplay with the visual, intuitive right brain. Children need only realize that drama is fun, will allow them to experience many things, and can help teach them valuable skills (see *Four C's*, page 37).

When do I schedule drama?

Any time! Use it in any part of your curriculum and as an extra activity designed to improve classroom cooperation, individual responsibility, leadership and creativity. Should you have a resource person or drama specialist, that time will be scheduled but be willing to try new things and involve yourself with the action. Have fun!

How do I integrate drama into academic areas of the curriculum?

The book contains suggestions and activities for each subject area. These are only the *tip of the iceberg* but will give you a start. You'll think of countless ideas yourself and I suggest you start a notebook or put your ideas on 3x5 inch cards to be filed. Use your student's imagination. It is boundless!

With so much emphasis on academics, can I justify drama as part of my curriculum?

Yes, more and more schools are adopting drama as a viable part of the curriculum.[1] Teachers consistently report that dramatic involvement brings their class together, improves self-discipline, and seems to give children purpose and direction. Consequently, it increases their enthusiasm for academic achievement.

What about discipline? Won't children get out of control, and if they do, what's the best way to deal with it?

All teachers have ways, so use whatever works best for you. I like to have all ages get *Five Things Ready* (page 36) before beginning any activity. The emphasis on *consideration* seems to help and this remains my main tool for control, especially consideration for each other's *feelings*. Feelings are emphasized as the most important thing any of us has, and therefore great care must be taken so that no one gets his or her feelings hurt. I compliment good behavior and ignore, as much as possible, those who try to draw attention negatively. It is helpful to encourage children to do so as well. Exclusion is the only punishment used and that is made as short as possible. The self-discipline that drama promotes is one of the main benefits. Children universally love the activities, so motivation is a big part of the key to a good working atmosphere.

How do I begin?

I'll divide this answer into three groups; kindergarten, primary and secondary.

For smaller children it helps to have them sit on the floor, as close together as possible. I start with *Five Things Ready* (page 36), explaining as I go and *wait* until all are ready. I introduce myself and say a few personal things and go around the group, just having them say their name and, "Hi!" We talk a little about drama, what it is, and how much fun we can have if we follow the one rule — *to be considerate* — especially of feelings.

Copy Me (page 12) is a good way to begin, sometimes even choosing leaders from the group to take my place while I look on to watch for good copiers, explaining that this requires concentration, which is one of the things we learn to do in drama.

The next really critical area is pantomime and I briefly explain that this means making No Sound. It seems helpful to start with the most dramatic, by saying, "Without making a sound, *scream*." Wonder of wonders, they cooperate and the rare time that a little rebel is heard, I briefly explain again, no sound! and repeat the exercise. Next, I'll ask them to cry, laugh, talk, ask questions, argue, all, with no sound. Once this is well established I may ask them to stand up, stamp their feet and clap their hands, all with no sound, adding the instructions, "Don't touch anything but the floor!" Moving around the room, the possibilities are endless. For ideas, use *Emotions* (page 19), *Animals* (page 1), *Places* (page 97), *Objects* (page 92), *Hands* (page 46), *Verbs* (page 155) and, eventually, *Situations* (page 127).

Some early games and exercises which are appropriate and fun are: *Listening* (page 73), *Five Senses* (page 34), *Keeping Your Cool* (page 69), *Introductions* (page 60), *Mirror* (page 86), *Change Three* (page 7), and *Who Started the Motion* (page 165).

Later activities can be designed to your individual needs and the class capability, as this varies from year to year.

For the first session in Primary classes, I usually have them remain in their seats, but ask that their desks be cleared so they won't be tempted to get distracted. I wait for the *Five Things Ready* (page 36) and then either begin with *Copy Me* (page 12), or *Introductions* (page 60 or 62). The rule to *be considerate* can be stated or guessed at (see *Four C's,* page 37) but it needs to be established early on. We discuss pantomime and *Hands* (page 46) is a good activity to start with. I use much of the same procedure described for the younger ones but may add *Introduction Exercise* (page 60) to give them the experience early on of communicating with an audience. All of the pantomime and speech activities are fun for this age group. Story telling and skits can be used in a flexible way to fit into subject areas. Poetry makes a great topic at any point and there are a number of favorite games and activities listed in the Table of Contents. Children at this age love doing performances and teachers universally say, "It was worth the effort!" These shows can be as simple or as elaborate as you wish.

Secondary classes still need the *Five Things Ready* (page 36) and it is equally important to establish other rules early on. The one rule, to *be considerate*, is sufficient for it really covers all things. I always discuss the *Four C's* (page 37) with this age group (even if they've had it before). *Keep Your Cool* (page 69) is a never ending favorite and a real help with discipline. Pantomime warm-ups can be used at any time, with *bringing to life* a technique promoting spontaneity. My goal, at this level, is to promote individual creativity, leadership and cooperative effort. Role plays are excellent, as are any small skit type activities. Extemporaneous speaking (*Spontaneous Speaking*, page 144) produces confidence and there are a number of activities described that help with this skill. Memorization, script writing and acting are also appropriate and beneficial. My feeling is that these lessons need not be done in a sequential order but used in a more spontaneous and individual way, based on the teacher's needs, energy and desire.

---

[1] Cook, Wayne D., *Center Stage, a Curriculum for the Performing Arts*, Dale Seymour Publisher, 1993 (Polly Erion, consultant writer)—adopted in Texas as part of the curriculum.

Ample white space is provided in this book for your notes and ideas.

TABLE OF CONTENTS

ANIMALS

GRADES: K–8

TYPE OF ACTIVITY: Full group, active, pantomime with activity; bringing to *life*

GOALS:
1. To interpret animal's behavior and feel a relationship to animals
2. To practice pantomiming
3. To develop creativity, originality and imagination

READINESS: All types of animals, fish and fowl provide excellent pantomime material. All ages can participate in this game. Portraying animals is used in Greek myths, folk tales from other countries and naturally any fairy tales, so it is well for them to have practice. Discuss how animals have feelings too, and treating them kindly helps us understand our own natures. Ask for typical movements which different animals make.

PROCEDURE:
1. Review pantomime, freeze, and bringing to life, appropriate to age group.

2. Call out different animals and let the group pantomime being the animal, such as:

a	anteater
b	bear, bat, bird, bunny, butterfly
c	cat, canary, cow, chick, crow
d	dog, donkey, duck, dragon, deer
e	eagle, elephant
f	fox, fish
g	giraffe, gopher, goat
h	hippopotamus, horse
i	iguana
k	kangaroo, kitten
l	lamb, lion
m	mole, mouse, monkey
o	ostrich, ox, opossum

p	puppy, panther, pig
q	quail
r	rabbit, rooster, rhinoceros
s	snake, shark, sheep, squirrel
t	tiger, turtle
w	whale,zebra

VARIATION A:	Freeze group and bring one at a time to life.
VARIATION B:	Divide group into audience/actor and have group performing think of an animal and act it out for group to guess.
VARIATION C:	Give the letters of the alphabet something beginning with a 'B', 'C,' 'E,' etc.
VARIATION D:	"Think of what you would like to be if you could be any animal." Come to life on signal.

EVALUATION: Appropriate for any age; excellent to loosen children up.

AUDIENCE/ACTOR

GRADES: K–8

TYPE OF ACTIVITY: Full group to emphasize consideration for both audience and actors

GOALS:
1. To learn to be an attentive audience
2. To learn how to give constructive and considerate comments
3. To dramatize with an awareness of the responsibility involved in entertaining an audience
4. To provide an interesting activity which involves everyone at all times

READINESS: Discuss the importance of being a good audience with full attention on the actors, and that they are to try to notice details and good concentration, as comments will be made after each mini-performance. Impress the children with their responsibility as actors: to *be considerate*, and entertain the audience and *not* only themselves.

PROCEDURE:
1. Divide the class into half — audience/actor. It is helpful at this time to use some signal, either hand or piano, for the children to learn how to go up on the stage, how to stand and prepare themselves for *acting*. For instance, ask the designated group to look at your hands. When you turn them over, they are to rise simultaneously. The child on the right will then lead them up onto the stage. It is sometimes fun to suggest that the leader do a funny walk for all to copy.

2. Designate a line for them to stand on, and request that they immediately assume *first position*, which is standing straight, on two feet, hands behind their backs or at their sides. *Second position* is with the hands in front, and this position is used when speaking.

3. If introductions or solo numbers are to be done, point out that they must hold *first position* when not performing so they won't call attention to themselves and distract the audience from focusing on the *actor.* Sometimes they are all acting simultaneously, and then this technique is not required.

4. Children can be asked to do any of the pantomime activities, and are even frozen and brought to life when appropriate.

SPECIAL NEEDS: For this activity it is not necessary to insist that everyone go up on stage. When the division is boy/girl there is more universal participation.

EVALUATION: Audience/actor can be used at any time, as the children never tire of it, and continue to benefit each time they do it.

BOOK REPORTS

GRADES: 3–8

TYPE OF ACTIVITY: In-class activity involving summary skills, speaking, and acting

GOALS:
1. To motivate children to learn to summarize effectively
2. To develop story telling ability
3. To give children acting opportunities
4. To stimulate interest in reading particular books

READINESS: This procedure involving drama will help children with the all important skill of making book reports. The spontaneous summaries are a delightful way for them to discover that this approach is fun and needn't be painful. Sometimes it is appropriate to discuss summaries before starting: how they need to briefly include *who, what, when,* and *where.*

PROCEDURE:
1. Ask for volunteers to tell about a book which they have read and enjoyed. Select someone to come up and share. If they have the book, it can be brought up and displayed.

2. Ask for the title, author, degree of difficulty, number of pages, and what they especially liked about the book.

3. Request a *very brief* summary of the book, saying things like,
   - "Just give us a general idea."
   - "Don't worry about the details."
   - "Make it simple. Just one or two sentences."

4. Once the summary is completed, ask for a description of a little scene from the book. If it appears that you have a confident story teller, ask him to cast his scene quickly and tell each child his character.
   - "You are Tommy, a five year old brat."

- "You are a crabby mother."
- "You are an old beggar."

5. The story teller is left as free as possible to make his selections, even requesting children to play the part of trees, doors, tables, whatever! The scene is held together by the child telling the story, possibly side-directed by the teacher to keep the focus on being considerate to the audience.

6. Each child is given only five to eight minutes *so the others get a chance.* Evaluations are brief, constructive, and positive.

VARIATION A: Make it an assignment that each child *write* a one minute summary of his book. This may be done as homework, or you can give the class five to ten minutes of class time. The summaries are handed in and selection is made on the basis of clarity, or, naturally, where it might especially benefit a particular child.

VARIATION B: Put the children in groups and let them come up with an *agreed upon* book and scene from the book.

VARIATION C: Ask that the children illustrate their scene. "A picture is worth a thousand words." This allows opportunity for further creativity.

EVALUATION: Dramatic book reports are fun, stimulating, and educational. They are fun because the children love selecting and acting out a favorite scene from the book. They are stimulating, because others are encouraged to read the book. They are educational for several reasons: most notably children are taught to think in terms of a one to two sentence summary, a very significant skill to develop as early as possible.

This activity is successful at any grade level from third on up.

CHANGE THREE

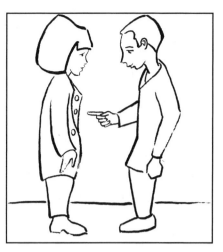

GRADES: K–3

TYPE OF ACTIVITY: A game done in pairs, which improves observational abilities

GOALS:
1. To promote good feelings
2. To help them get better acquainted
3. To improve observation abilities
4. To give an opportunity for fun and frolic

READINESS: Discuss what a difference it makes when we really *look* at something. Ask the children to look very carefully at you and describe some details. Point out some objects in the room and do the same thing. Stress the importance of developing this skill.

PROCEDURE:
1. Pair the children off and then ask each pair to observe each other carefully. They are to notice things such as how their partners are dressed, the color and style of hair, color of eyes, expression of face, and so on.

2. They are to decide who is number one and who is number two. Ask all the *ones* to raise their hands, then all the *twos*.

3. Ask number ones to stand, for they are to be the first observers. They are told that they have one minute to look at their partners *very carefully,* for when they return, their partner will have changed three things. They are again instructed to look at such things as their partner's hair, shoes, how their shirts are buttoned, etc.

4. The observers are then told to come away and turn their backs while the partners change three things. Two or three minutes are generally long enough for the partners to accomplish this task.

5. Give the count down backwards from ten to one. Partners re-

turn and try to find the three things. If they do, both children in the pair are to stand. If they can't find the three things, their partners tell them. Next, the roles are reversed until the game is completed.

SPECIAL NEEDS: Children with special needs or problems can effectively be paired with an especially considerate child and receive needed positive reinforcement.

EVALUATION: This game has a special quality about it. It is personal, involves creative thinking and observation. Younger children especially love it, but it can be very enjoyable for older children also.

CONCENTRATION

GRADES: 1–8

TYPE OF ACTIVITY: A game involving all or part of the class. Helps develop memory and conceptual understanding of grammar, vocabulary, and related areas of learning.

MATERIALS:
1. Durable piece of cardboard, about 3 x 5 feet
2. Sixteen 3 x 5 inch cards
3. Any number of smaller cards: 2½ x 4½ inch
4. Paper clips

GOALS:
1. To improve memory
2. To learn subject matter with the use of a game
3. To help with concentration for a purpose

READINESS:
1. Print or attach the letters "CONCENTRATION" across the top of the piece of cardboard.
2. Print the first 16 letters of the alphabet in large, bold characters on the 3 x 5 cards, one letter to a card. Attach these to the board with tape, taping the top of the card to the board so that the card can be lifted up to look underneath.

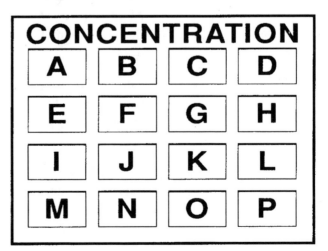

3. Using the smaller cards in pairs, print information for matching, such as:

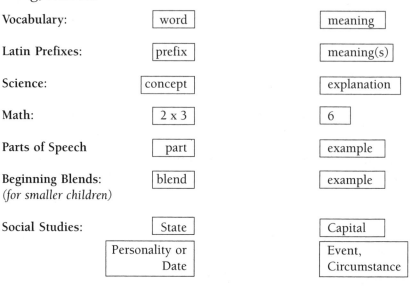

Vocabulary: word meaning

Latin Prefixes: prefix meaning(s)

Science: concept explanation

Math: 2 x 3 6

Parts of Speech part example

Beginning Blends: blend example
(for smaller children)

Social Studies: State Capital
Personality or Date Event, Circumstance

4. Select eight pairs of these information cards, and using paper clips, attach one to the back of the letter cards on the board, so that when the letter cards are lifted, the words on the information cards can be read. This should be done prior to starting the game, without the students watching.

Caution the students that no signals or help must be given to the team members as they participate, or they lose their turn. Encourage dramatization of the word, prefix, etc., as it helps the child internalize its meaning.

PROCEDURE:

1. Put the students in teams, using whatever selection method you prefer, and appoint someone to be record keeper.

2. Have the teams agree (or else you decide) prior to starting the game that, upon finding a pair, the team's turn continues, or that each team alternate turns, regardless of whether a match is made.

3. The first participant chooses two of the letter cards, such as A and K. Those two cards are lifted for all to see. If the pairs match, that team gets to keep the information cards and is awarded two points.

4. If the pair does not match, the students attempt to remember what was under each card so that eventually all matches can be made.

5. The game continues until all matches have been made and all 16 letters have no cards under them. The team with the most cards wins.

VARIATION A: Let the children play it in pairs on their own, with a third child as record keeper and card turner.

VARIATION B: Play boys against girls; it is always a challenge and fun.

Curriculum Homework:

Have the children make up their own as an assignment.

EVALUATION: Children never seem to tire of this game, and ask for it repeatedly. One of the children can play teacher and arrange the cards for the next game. This same idea can be used for literally any conceptual learning.

COPY ME

GRADES: K-8

TYPE OF ACTIVITY: Full group participation with one leader at a time; opportunity for all to try leadership role

GOALS:
1. To emphasize leadership qualities
2. To help children concentrate and focus
3. To calm children and achieve discipline
4. To give an opportunity for fun and innovative voice and pantomime

READINESS: Discuss the meaning of the word *concentrate* and point out how this ability to think about one thing *only will* make it easier to learn most *anything:* baseball, tennis, math, or *drama.* Draw out comments from the children to reinforce this concept.

PROCEDURE:
1. Simply ask the children to start *copying* by saying "Copy me." Stand or sit where they can see you.

2. Make the movements simple and slow at first, and if someone is not following, look directly at that person and direct energy to him.

3. Begin using your voice any way you like:
   - "Hi," soft and loud
   - "It's good to be here."
   - "You all look funny," etc.

4. Choose someone else to be leader, then watch the group carefully, commenting on good concentration.

5. Walk in front of the group and point out that they need to focus only on their leader, not me.

6. Have the leader choose someone else, and so forth.

SPECIAL NEEDS: Children handicapped in one way or another often make great leaders for this activity. Even the shyest child will come up if approached positively. It helps to assist in this case with directions such as: "Lift one hand; Pat your head; Say 'Hi!' "

EVALUATION: This game is an all-time favorite. The children never tire of it, and the value is obvious. It has a remarkable calming effect when used for that purpose. It is also a good way to teach choral lines, proper enunciation, and *fun* characterizations. It can be used before shows to calm children, and often to begin shows.

COPY THE LEADER

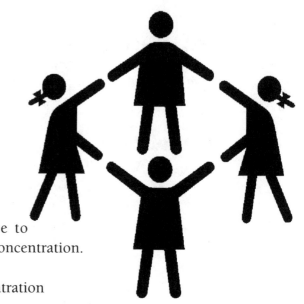

GRADES: K–8

TYPE OF ACTIVITY: Small group exercise to help teamwork and concentration.

GOALS:
1. To promote concentration
2. To promote leadership
3. To involve all the children as organizers

READINESS: Discuss the value of concentration and what it involves to be a good leader. Try to bring out the awareness that a *leader* needs to be considerate and aware of the members' ability to follow.

PROCEDURE:
1. Put all the children in groups of five or six and direct them to sit in a circle.

2. Direct one child in each group to be the *leader*, and the rest are to follow. Frequently, music can be used so that they start moving when the music starts and freeze when it stops.

3. Go around to each group and tap a new person to be leader, or else call out a name. Eventually have them all stand and do their movements standing.

VARIATION A: Use a variety of music to encourage different types of movement. The children are instructed to freeze when the music stops.

VARIATION B: Let the children stand and follow one another, requesting that they leave a space of at least two feet between each child. Encourage large movements.

EVALUATION: This is an excellent activity, as it promotes some exciting and creative movements from the children. It is very helpful in promoting cooperative effort and developing leadership.

DIALOGUE IN PAIRS

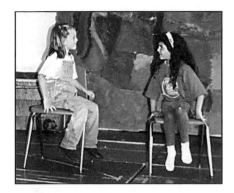

GRADES: 2–8

TYPE OF ACTIVITY: Verbal, done in pairs with opportunity for all to participate

GOALS:
1. To provide an opportunity for acting and reversing roles
2. To help shy children gain confidence
3. To promote improvisational techniques
4. To have fun

READINESS: Discuss the meaning of *role,* i.e., playing a part and attempting to make it as near to real life as possible. Talk about how, in this exercise, roles will be instantly reversed.

PROCEDURE:
1. Have the children form a line with those who wish to participate.

2. The first two children seat themselves and prepare to take their respective roles.

3. After a designated signal they reverse roles; or have the child on the right go to the end of the line and the child on the left take his place while the first person in the line moves to the then empty seat.

4. Possible pairs:
   a. Santa and little child
   b. Dr. (psychiatrist) and patient
   c. Teacher or principal and troublesome student
   d. *Weirdo* (nonconformist) and *straight* (conformist). The *straight* person is instructed to be honest and the *weirdo* tries to annoy with bizarre behavior
   e. Parent and child (discussing any appropriate or amusing subject)
   f. Parent and teacher with a troublesome conference

g. Employer needing to fire an employee

h. Policeman and robber

i. Storekeeper and thief

j. King or queen and servant

k. Attorney and defendant (they love to ham it up)

l. Ask them to think of their own

5. Signalling for change can be done by the teacher, or regulated by the children's own discretion, as long as they don't take up too much time.

EVALUATION: This activity is *a favorite,* and promotes much creativity. It can be used effectively as a performance piece.

DIRECTION TAKING

GRADES: 2–8

TYPE OF ACTIVITY: Small or large group activity to improve concentration and memory

GOALS:
1. To improve memory
2. To help children with listening skills
3. To learn key terms involving directions, such as horizontal vertical, every other, right, left, measurements, etc.

READINESS: Discuss the difficulties one can have taking tests and understanding directions; how the mind can blank out and *freeze*. Try to reassure the children that this ability, like any other, requires practice. Emphasize the game aspect of this activity, and that we only look for the number of things done correctly.

PROCEDURE:
1. Give the following preliminary instructions:
   a. Sit up with *Five Things Ready* (page 36).
   b. Put your pencil one inch above your paper in a horizontal position.
   c. Listen to *all* the directions.
   d. Wait a few seconds after the directions are given to let the words *settle in*, then pick up your pencil and do the best you can. Skip those things you don't understand or remember, and do the rest.
   e. When you finish, turn your paper over and draw a picture.

2. Directions can involve anything, such as:
   a. Write your name and the date in the upper right hand corner.
   b. Make a check in the lower left hand corner.

c. Start numbering on the second horizontal blue line; put your numerals directly to the left of the red vertical line; skip every other blue line, number to 10, circling every even number, etc.

d. Draw a circle in the lower right hand corner, having the diameter of two inches.

e. Continue with a variety of directions, gradually increasing the number and complexity.

3. Once this part has been completed, any little *test* can be done, such as spelling, mental math, draw the points of the compass, formulas for math, Latin prefixes, or vocabulary — anything one wishes to emphasize.

SPECIAL NEEDS: If this activity is too difficult for a particular child, allow him to quietly observe until he feels confident enough to attempt the exercise.

EVALUATION: The important aspect of this exercise is the concentration required. Children love it, see their own improvement, and come to fear *tests* and *direction-taking* less and less.

EMOTIONS/FEELINGS

GRADES: K–8

TYPE OF ACTIVITY: Whole group activity using pantomime and voice

GOALS: 1. To promote awareness and expression of children's own feelings

2. To practice controlling emotions

3. To begin learning the essence of drama/acting

4. To have fun

READINESS: Discuss how we respond to emotions; demonstrate. Bring out awareness that children know *true feelings.*

PROCEDURE: 1. Call out feelings; children move around, pantomime, acting out each feeling.

A   angry, ashamed, ambitious, authoritative, aggressive, astonished, awful, annoyed, amused, alert, afraid, achieving, appealing, affectionate, aloof, admiring, artful, achy, alive, athletic, astounded, anxious, amazed, active, attractive, antagonistic, abrupt, adorable, agreeable, animated, absurd, amazed, aghast, addled…

B   big, blue, bored, brave, beautiful, busy, babbling, boastful, bewildered, brilliant, better, babyish, balanced, bitter, blank, blistering, blunt, bulging, beastly, brutal, bright, bold, brusque, brash…

C   cold, clean, curious, confused, clumsy, cheerful, carried away, crabby, cute, crafty, cranky, carefree, careful, courageous, cross, cruel, crude, crouching, crushed, crotchety, crumby, charming, cramped, calm, childish, considerate, concealed, colorful, craving, constructive, commanding…

D   distinguished, determined, depressed, dumb, discouraged, disturbed, dreary, different, dirty, deserted, daring, dull, drowsy, dreamy, droopy, dismayed, daring, dizzy, disappointed, disgusted, dramatic, decisive, dropped, drunk, dejected, delightful, disgraced, disguised, dissatisfied, destructive...

E   excited, ecstatic, energetic, eager, easy, equal, enthused, enhanced, engulfed, enormous, enthralled, elevated, elastic, electric, elderly, eerie, effeminate, exacting, exaggerated, exasperated, exhilarated, exonerated, exotic...

F   funny, fierce, frazzled, frightened, faint, facetious, fair, failure, faint-hearted, famished, fairy-like, fascinated, fearful, feathery, feeble, ferocious, fervent, flabby, feverish, flighty, furtive, filthy, first-rate, fishy, flaming, fleeting, fleshy, flippant, flexible, flouncing, flirtatious, fluid...

G   gay, guilty, glad, great, grouchy, goofy, greedy, gross, gruesome, good, gentle, gorgeous, gloomy, groovy, grumpy, grateful, gleeful, gigantic, gambling, gangling, gauche, genial, ghastly, ghostly, grandiose, grown-up...

H   happy, hot, hungry, heavy, hysterical, horrified, hurt, helpful, hypnotic, homesick, horrible, hairy, hopeless, harmless, hateful, humorous, humiliated, hilarious, homely, horrifying, hip, haughty, honest, hollow, hesitant, heroic, hurried, humdrum, humane...

I   innocent, ignored, irritated, itchy, idiotic, injured, imaginative, important, impatient, icky, intelligent, irresistible, independent, indignant, icy, ignorant, immobile, imitative, improper, impressive, inconspicuous...

J   joyful, jumpy, juvenile, jittery, jealous, jostling, jovial, jazzy, jubilant, jumbled, judgmental, juggling, just...

K   kingly, kidnapped, knavish, knotty, knowledgeable, kittenish...

L   loving, loyal, limp, lecherous, lithe, late, large, lackadaisical, laborious, laggard, landing, languid, lascivious, low, latent, lean, lazy, lethal, learned, lethargic, liberal, light, lifeless, in limbo, lingering, locked...

M   mean, mousy, mirthful, magnificent, mad, machine-like, magnetic, magnanimous, magnified, microscopic, malevolent, malicious, maladjusted, malnourished, mangled, mangy, martyred, massive, mellow, menacing, melancholy, metallic, metamorphosed, mighty, militant, mischievous, modest, mortified, moody...

N   nervous, naughty, nice, neat, nasty, naive, natural, natty, near-sighted, neighborly, negative, negligent, neutral, neurotic, niggardly, noble, nonsensical, normal, nosy, notable, notorious, noticeable…

O   old, ornery, organized, obese, obedient, obnoxious, ordinary, offensive, old-fashioned, omnipotent, optimistic, opinion-ated, orderly, original, ostracized, outgoing, outstretched, owly, overtired, overworked…

P   pretty, puzzled, proud, poor, pleased, peppy, perplexed, playful, peculiar, patriotic, pacified, pained, pampered, paranoid, paralyzed, parallel, perpendicular, particular, participating, patient, popular, peculiar, peaceful, penniless, persnickety, persecuted, philanthropic, phenomenal, picayune, possessive…

Q   quiet, questionable, quibbling, quick, quivering, questioning…

R   rushed, regal, rotten, respectful, rejected, romantic, rich, ravenous, rambunctious, resentful, rude, rabid, radiant, rakish, rangy, rapid, rascally, rash, realistic, rebellious, reduced, reformed, refreshed, renowned, resilient, restless, restrained, revolting, righteous, riotous, rosy, rubbery..

S   sparkling, stupid, sympathetic, sick, silly, strange, scared, soft, strong, sorry, shaky, snoopy, stunned, sleepy, sloppy, stuck-up, steaming, stuck, squirmy, shy, small, smart, superb, stuffed, starving, satisfied, sarcastic, slithery, sticky, strong, sweet, shocked, special, sore, suspicious, starving, skeptical, sly, sneaky, sad, surprised…

T   tired, terrific, terrible, thirsty, terrified, thoughtful, thin, tense, tender, timid, thrilled, tough, troubled, tiny, taut, tardy, tattling, tearful, thick, thorough, threatening, together, tight, tipsy, tongue-tied, trampled, tremendous, tenderhearted, tame…

U   ugly, unwanted, unhappy, uneasy, upset, unbelievable, unconscious, unfriendly, unhealthy, up-to-date, unique, unaware, unconquerable, unruly, unselfish…

V   vain, vulgar, vicious, vague, vaporized, variegated, valuable, vehement, velvety, verbose, vexatious, vigorous, visionary, virulent, vital, vacuous…

W   wobbly, warm, wishywashy, weary, warlike, wanting, weightless, waiting…

Y   young, youthful, yielding, yawning, yellow…

Z   zany, zooming, zesty, zealous, zig-zaggy…

VARIATION A: Freeze and bring to life.

VARIATION B: Use for vocabulary building.

VARIATION C: Divide class in half. Observe and comment.

EVALUATION: Children of all ages never tire of this activity, and it serves as an invaluable warm-up.

ENUNCIATION CAN BE FUN

GRADES: K–8

TYPE OF ACTIVITY: Training designed to improve all aspects of speech and communication

GOALS:

1. To improve enunciation and clarity of delivery

2. To help children become aware of the rhythmic quality of speech and the emphasis that is required on certain syllables

3. To improve breathing techniques

4. To encourage greater mobility of the mouth and tongue in order to clarify sounds and make them more distinguishable

5. To make children aware of the subtle *group feeling* coming from reciting together

6. To provide a pleasurable experience for children to work on the important skill of verbal communication and dramatic emphasis

READINESS: Stress the importance of good speech, and that correct breathing is the foundation, the same as it is of good health. Most of us have lazy and indifferent enunciation, so our words come out garbled or unclear. Point out that correct speech helps spelling, and many other aspects of their daily lives.

PROCEDURE:

1. Start with some exercises to loosen up the body:

   a. Everyone stand and stretch;

   b. Roll your heads like a big knuckle, one direction and then another;

   c. Put your legs about a foot apart and flop down, nice and loose;

   d. Hum. Feel the vibration in your nose and go up and down the scale;

e. Do some tongue stretches. Try to touch your nose, your chin, click it inside your mouth, etc.;

f. Yawn, without sound, and then with sound;

g. Sigh, as this is the ideal breath.

2. Have them do some exercises to help with greater mobility and elasticity of the mouth and lips:

a. Put your lips as for whistling and blow gently;

b. Without breath, make the shape of:

ee…oo…ee…oo…etc.
ah…uh…ah…uh…etc.;

c. Drop your jaw loosely;

d. Flick the tongue lightly and quickly with the sound of "la, la, la, la, la." Change the speed and do sometimes with breath and sometimes without;

e. Say sounds of *bmmmm, pmmmm, tnnn, dnnn*, etc., and make the sound continuous with the lips closed throughout. Do the same thing with *gong, gng, king, kng*, etc.

3. The following exercise can be put on the board and done as a group to further the sharp and clear enunciation, rhythm in speaking, and group awareness:

<u>dr</u>	<u>dr</u>	<u>dr</u>	<u>dr</u>
<u>dr</u>, dr	<u>dr</u>, dr	<u>dr</u>, dr	<u>dr</u>
<u>dr</u>, dr, dr	<u>dr</u>, dr, dr	<u>dr</u>, dr, dr	<u>dr</u>
<u>dr</u>, dr, dr,	<u>dr</u>, dr, dr, dr	<u>dr</u>, dr, dr, dr	<u>dr</u>

(*Make sure that they pronounce this as "<u>dru</u>" and not "<u>dur</u>".*)

They are to say this as a chorus, with the teacher directing.

They can also try it alone, and are usually very successful.

Any blends can be used, such as: tr, spr, br, gl gr, ick, and so forth.

4. Some further activities are as follows:

a. Say, "Ho…ho…ho" and let it drop out of your throat. Pretend you are pulling the sound out and stretch it as far as you can;

b. Make some siren sounds — soft and then loud. Blow the roof off (assuming that you are in a place where this is possible and will not disturb anyone);

c. Sing the ABC song, and exaggerate all the letters — soft and then loud;

d. Pantomime singing like an opera star, and then like a rock star. Now, you have your choice to sing your name like one or the other, adding anything about yourself that you like. (Each child does this as a solo.)

EVALUATION: These activities are really beneficial to children of any age. Some classes are more receptive than others, but once the class gets in the spirit of the thing, fun is had by all. These exercises provide excellent reinforcement for phonics and spelling.

ENVIRONMENT

GRADES: K–8

TYPE OF ACTIVITY: This lesson includes a number of ideas for ways to incorporate an appreciation of the natural word around us into drama activities which fit into the curriculum.

GOALS:

1. To stimulate their natural curiosity

2. To help children realize how dependent we all are on a healthy environment.

3. To make children aware of ways in which they can help.

4. To encourage an appreciation of the beauties of nature.

READINESS: Environment is defined as all of the surrounding conditions and influences that affect the development of a living thing. Encourage the children to come up with as many ideas of their own as to some of these conditions and influences. Naturally it depends on the age group as to how detailed you want to get. There could be some discussion of the above goals at this time.

MATERIALS: Any natural items such as rocks, leaves, nuts, berries, fruit, vegetables, acorns, pictures, videos, live animals and plants. Magazine pictures, stories, poems, scripts or anything appropriate to the example selected.

PROCEDURE: Choose one of the following examples depending on objectives or needs.

EXAMPLE A: Play any of the Five Senses Games (page 34), only be sure to use only natural objects. Discuss how animals and even plants use their senses. Put the children in small groups and have them make up little mini-dramas having to do with one of the five senses.

EVALUATION: These lessons or games are wonderful for any age group and help reinforce learning through the use of the five senses.

EXAMPLE B: Have a stack of 3 x 5 cards and have on each card a place such as; the forest, the beach, the mountain and so forth. Children can individually volunteer to come up, draw a card and then pantomime the "place" or small groups can be given a card and think of a way to demonstrate where they are as a group project.

EVALUATION: An especially valuable "mixer" and helps encourage an interest in the environment.

EXAMPLE C: Make a writing project with the environment as the subject. Encourage them to emphasize conservation but also leave it open so that any creative effort will be acceptable. This could be prose or poetry. Their writings can be used for oral reading practice.

EVALUATION: Some of our best shows have been done this way and came entirely from the students.

EXAMPLE D: Plan a performance based on ecology and preserving the beauty of the Earth.

Gonna Have An Earth Day, by Mary Lynn Lightfoot*

EVALUATION: This is an excellent musical designed to appeal to both younger and older students. The show is both informative and upbeat, giving an honest look at the problems we face and showing parents and children how they can make a difference.

EXAMPLE E: Choose some music appropriate to the subject and encourage children to contribute ideas for dramatization and art work.

Recycle, by Kirby Shaw
This Pretty Planet, by Audrey Snyder
The Earth Celebration, by Sheri Porterfield & Audrey Snyder*

EVALUATION: These are all marvelous open-minded musical stimulants to creativity. Students are especially enthusiastic about spearheading an awareness of environmental concerns. Artwork related to the subject has been phenomenal and even won prizes.

* Pepper, Classroom and Performance Catalog, 1-800-345-6296

FABLES

GRADES: 1–8

TYPE OF ACTIVITY: Dramatic and musical presentation of *Æsop's Fables* and other fables

MATERIALS: *Æsop's Fables*, Gilberts Musical *Æsop's Fables* (any book on fables)

GOALS:
1. To improve teamwork and the awareness of good sportsmanship

2. To gain understanding through the discussion of fables and the appropriate morals

3. To do some real life dramas which demonstrate the morals

4. To gain from group planning, small group participation and informal presentations which enable children to learn from each other

5. To give opportunity for solo work for talented children

6. To increase each child's confidence through participation in a dramatic presentation

READINESS: This activity may include the entire class, although some children will be chosen for solo parts and time must be allowed for individual work. Solo parts are selected on a basis of talent, cooperation, and consideration. If this is the first drama activity for the class, start with several beginning exercises. Emphasize frequently that good sportsmanship, both in and out of class, is a key requirement for any performance part — lead or support — as they are all equally important.

It is important for the children to feel positive about what they are doing. Whenever possible, include all class members, using them as trees, chairs, doors, houses — literally any inanimate object. They all love to do this, and compliments should be freely given for the best *freeze*.

PROCEDURE:

1. Read or tell several fables, and then ask the children if they remember any. Have a discussion about how fables are stories which teach a lesson, often by using animals and things in nature, such as the wind and the sun, to behave like humans in order to demonstrate these lessons.

2. A discussion about how these fables can be applied to real life can be done at this time, or it can be done later.

3. The next step is to have the children pantomime the characters in the fable, and also to *become* various objects and things, such as trees, rocks wind, sun, etc. At first this can be a group exercise, and they are reminded not to look at or to touch one another, as that would be inconsiderate and interfere with concentration.

4. The class can then be divided in half, with one half becoming the actors and the other half the audience. The audience needs to give its full attention to the actors, and the actors now need to be aware that they must be considerate to the audience and make their actions clearly visible, audible and understandable. Ask some questions that are designed so that the comments will be positive, such as,

   - "Who was concentrating particularly well?"
   - "What things were brought to life for you?"
   - "Which children showed their feelings with their entire body?"

   This critical evaluation should be done with care so that the comments do not become personal or embarrassing. They should be made along the line of:

   - "I would like it better if it was louder;"
   - "I would like it to be slower so I could understand;"
   - "It would be better if they didn't turn their backs."

5. Select the storyteller first, and then choose the actors, or have the storyteller pick the actors. Change several times so as many children as possible get a chance to try several roles.

6. Organize the children in small groups and let them plan on their own.

VARIATION A: Capture real life dramas which emerge from the children themselves. Have the children work in small groups to dramatize these little stories. This encourages critical thinking, problem solving, leadership qualities, and sportsmanship.

VARIATION B: Use Margaret Wardlaw Gilbert's *Æsop's Fables*. These musical fables are excellent, easily learned, wonderful to dramatize, and ones which have been used a number of times for shows and presentations.

VARIATION C: Have your students write their own fables.

VARIATION D: Emphasize artwork by having the children illustrate the fables, make costumes and sets, and be as creative as possible.

SPECIAL NEEDS: Include all children. Often a particular fable suits a child with a disability or other problem, i. e., "Slow and steady wins the race," from *The Tortoise and the Hare*.

EVALUATION: Fables are wonderful for any age, from Kindergarten through 8th grade. They provide excellent related learning material. These little skits are very adaptable to small or large scale production.

FIVE REALITIES

GRADES: 3–8

TYPE OF ACTIVITY: A theater game which helps with improvisational acting skills, the *Freeze*, and teamwork.

GOALS:

1. To build those skills necessary for spontaneous and natural type acting

2. To provide a healthy and enjoyable way to build interaction between players

3. To learn how to give a variety of acting situations designed to entertain

4. To provide a cathartic release for children's inhibitions

READINESS: Discuss cooperation again, and how it will be necessary to both cooperate and to communicate in this exercise. The children must develop a sense of timing so that each scene is neither too long nor too short. Remind them that they must always be aware of the audience; that the selections are entertaining and considerate, so that the actors don't slip into entertaining themselves.

PROCEDURE:

1. It begins with one child starting a scene. A second child comes on and takes a Freeze. Both then Freeze.

2. The second child begins a totally new scene. The first child *joins in* once he understands where and who they are from the clues given.

3. A third child comes on after an appropriate time span and begins something entirely different, until all five have repeated this format.

4. Eventually the fifth child thinks of a reason to leave and the remaining children go back to the fourth scene.

5. The fourth child leaves after a bit and the remaining three go back to the third scene, and so forth until only the first child remains.

6. At this time he goes back to where he left off in the first scene.

SPECIAL NEEDS: This activity may be too difficult for some children, but they will have a lot of fun watching and offering ideas.

EVALUATION: This exercise takes practice, but is a favorite. Familiar fairy tales make an especially entertaining theme, but anything can be used, such as nursery rhymes, movies, books, places, or anything that strikes their fancy. Generally, this activity works best with children who have had a fair amount of other drama activities and have achieved a sufficient amount of concentration.

FIVE SENSES

GOALS: 1. To improve awareness of the use one can make of one's senses

2. To help children to *attend* to a specific thing

3. To use games which make learning fun

READINESS: Emphasize how important our five senses are and tell the children about real people who have lost key senses and compensated by using other senses, such as Helen Keller, Steve Hawkins, Wheelchair Olympics, and any other available examples.

PROCEDURE: 1. Sight:

Stress developing the ability to look for details, and how one's full attention is required. Some suggestions for games and activities which emphasize this sense are:

2. Hearing:

Emphasize the need to focus attention on this sense and try to shut out the other senses. Some excellent activities for this are:

3. Smell:

Discuss specific familiar smells and encourage the children to share, especially in regard to how we associate places and memories with distinctive odors (pine trees, earth, ocean, bread baking, etc.) Many animals have an incredibly developed sense of smell and use it in a variety of ways, from survival to communication:

a. What Is It?   (page 163)

b. Anatomy (see Science)   (page 120)

4. Taste:

Point out how the sense of taste and smell are related. Discuss the different types of tastes (sour, sweet, bitter, etc.)

a. What Is It?   (page 163)

b. Anatomy (see Science)   (page 120)

5. Touch:

Discuss how significantly the blind use their sense of touch to read Braille and for other purposes. Have the students experiment with feeling their own skin, the desk, their clothing, hair, etc.

a. What Is It?   K-8

b. Memory Game   K-8

Curriculum Connection:

1. Movies or video about famous people who have been successful despite their handicaps.

2. Have the children do reports on well-known people who have had to make exceptional use of one of their senses.

3. Put the children in small groups and have them come up with appropriate role plays emphasizing the five senses.

4. Ask for drawings or pictures from magazines depicting those things with a special taste or smell.

5. Ask children to bring in objects for discussion, games, and experimentation.

EVALUATION: The Five Senses are actually the foundation for all games and activities, and it should be impressed on the children that this is a lifelong process and that the better we develop our senses, the more capable we become.

FIVE THINGS READY

GRADES: K–8

TYPE OF ACTIVITY: Group exercise involving concentration

GOALS:
1. To gain full attention of the group
2. To help children learn to focus and concentrate
3. To create a calm and safe atmosphere

READINESS: The children should be seated first. Sometimes they are already at their desks, sometimes instructions require their being seated in front of a teacher, or to become an audience which may or may not involve walking into an auditorium or room. I ask that they walk with *dignity* as this helps *set the stage* for the five things.

PROCEDURE:
1. Simply say with authority, "Five things ready."

2. Explain the five things as:

   • You are sitting not touching anyone
   • Your hands are together
   • Your lips are closed
   • Your eyes are on me
   • Your ears are open

3. Wait until *all* have done this, repeating the step that may need emphasis, rather than calling out someone's name, ie.

   • "You are *sitting*, not *touching* anyone!"
   • "Your lips are closed."

4. When the children are fully ready, proceed with the lesson.

EVALUATION: This works for all ages and children seem to expect and like the calming effect it has on everyone. When they have nothing in their hands and no distractions, their energy becomes focused. In some cases we have added a *sixth* thing, a good attitude.

THE FOUR C'S

GRADES: K–8

TYPE OF ACTIVITY: Full group — guidelines for behavior and outlining of goals

GOALS:
1. To set the tone of the class towards self-discipline and consideration
2. To let children know that drama will help them in other areas and skills
3. To lead a discussion based on values

READINESS: Children should learn early on where your priorities are. When they understand that you really do care about their feelings and about creating a safe atmosphere, the tone of the class becomes focused and considerate.

PROCEDURE: There are four *C's* which will help them with drama. The first *C* has to do with the *only* rule.

1. Start by asking the class, "If you were to have only one rule which would make everything work, what would it be?"

   Suggestions will be forthcoming, and eventually it may be necessary to give hints, until we get — BE CONSIDERATE. Discuss how this relates to everything. Then ask, "What is the most precious thing we all have?" There will be bizarre answers, but it helps to put it on a personal level. "What sometimes gets hurt that you *never* get over?" *Feelings* will finally be the response.

2. Emphasize that we will be particularly considerate of one another's *feelings*, so put downs or disrespect will not be allowed. Children who forget will be left out of the activities for a short time.

3. Let them guess the three other *C's* which drama will help them with.

   • Concentration — to think of one thing only.

- Communication — to express yourself effectively.
- Cooperation — to be willing to share, be a good sport, and try things.

4. The result of the Four C's will be four more things beginning with C:

  - Confidence
  - Control
  - Creativity
  - Consistency

  As children come up with more ideas, they can be added to the list.

5. Ask for examples of the above if time permits.

EVALUATION: This whole procedure can be varied according to the age of the group, time allowed and overall purpose desired. I have found it a good way to start almost all classes.

FREEZE GAME

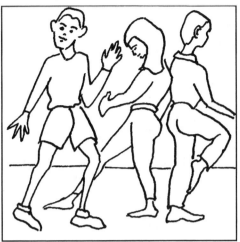

GRADES: K–8

TYPE OF ACTIVITY: Group activity done all together to emphasize the *Freeze*

GOALS:
1. To emphasize control
2. To have healthy competition so children can learn from one another
3. To have fun and allow activity which directs energy

READINESS: Discuss and demonstrate what it means to *Freeze*. The children need to understand that to be effective, there must be *no* movement, or as little as possible. Ask if anyone has seen this done; there is usually a wide range of response.

PROCEDURE:
1. Once children understand how to move about in pantomime, they can run, as long as they are considerate and do not bump into one another, staying in control of themselves.
2. Have a signal (a chord on the piano, voice, or turning off music) which will designate a *freeze*.

   After doing this several times, discuss briefly how a freeze takes all your energy, and the next freeze will be a little contest.
4. This time call those out who move, even slightly, asking them to just sit down where they are, or to go sit on the stage, or at one side of the room. They are told to watch the others.
5. Walk by the remaining *freezes*, clap your hands, even try to distract, pointing out their excellent concentration.
6. Finally, applaud for the remaining *freezes,* and begin again.

VARIATION A: **Elimination Freeze** — Sometimes this can be played as a game. The children are to find a *freeze* standing up by the count of ten. Then, one at a time, as they are caught moving, the children are called *out,* until the last one, who is the *winner.* This is a very good way to close a class period. It's fun to hand out notices or treats as each child is called *out.* The winner gets an extra treat.

VARIATION B: **Statue Freeze** — Ask the children to freeze as different characters, such as a snowman, a pirate, a cowboy, or a feeling, such as an angry statue, happy, etc.

EVALUATION: This is an all time great game, or activity, a favorite with all ages.

FREEZE IN PAIRS

GRADES: K–8

TYPE OF ACTIVITY: Theater game which encourages improvisation, creativity, and acting skills

GOALS:
1. To encourage spontaneity and improvisation
2. To try out acting skills on a casual basis
3. To encourage teamwork
4. To entertain an audience

READINESS: Emphasize teamwork and a *sense of timing*. Review the *Freeze* and suggest that the children try to vary the scenes as much as possible, keeping in mind that they are to entertain the audience as well as themselves.

PROCEDURE:
1. Two children are selected to go to the front of the room or stage, as the case may be, and one is designated to start a scene. The second child is to *join in,* but not *take over.*

2. They continue for a short time (30 seconds to a minute) until someone in the group calls out "Freeze!" They are both to Freeze and hold it, like a picture, until the child who called out the Freeze comes up and taps one of the children.

3. The *tapper* assumes the identical posture of the one he tapped, who leaves the scene and goes back to the group. The new person starts a different scene and the activity continues.

4. Sometimes have the group line up and take turns or tap a player and call out *Freeze!* Other times allow them to do it at random.

VARIATIONS:
1. Give them a subject like fairy tales, nursery rhymes, TV shows, locations, types of people, etc.

2. Give the first actor an imaginary object, such as a cup or ball. Each time the players change they are to imagine a new object and build their scene around it.

EVALUATION: This activity is for children who have had a fair amount of drama background or are quite mature. It is excellent to promote spontaneity in acting, characterizations, and good class tone. Encourage the actors to vary their scenes and share with the audience. This activity can be used as a performance piece. Younger children can be included, if there are mixed ages, as long as they are not pressured.

GRAVE DIGGER

GRADES: 2–8

TYPE OF ACTIVITY: Quiet game — large or small group

READINESS: Discuss the meaning of Zombie (corpse brought back to life by supernatural power)

PROCEDURE:

1. One child is chosen to be grave digger.

2. All the other children lie down flat — usually on their stomachs so their faces don't show. They freeze in that position.

3. The grave digger walks around and when he detects the slightest movement he taps that child to get up.

4. The child tapped becomes a Zombie and walks around slow and stiff-arms outstretched (designate an area away from the prone children so they don't get stepped on).

5. Children continue to become Zombies until the last one who is left then becomes the grave digger for the next game.

VARIATION: Children lie down on their back with their eyes open. The one standing goes from one to another trying to make them smile of laugh or move.

EVALUATION: A favorite game for most any time. It has a calming effect and children of all ages love it.

GUESS WHO?

GRADES: K–8

TYPE OF ACTIVITY: Group game which promotes voice control and emphasizes the sense of hearing. Fun anytime

GOALS:
1. To Improve listening skills
2. To learn to disguise voice
3. To help learn names
4. To promote good feelings
5. To provide a non-threatening opportunity for children to perform

READINESS: Demonstrate some different voices, even asking that they close their eyes to see if they can recognize the voice. Ask if they can identify familiar voices. Have them pantomime different characters, such as: witch, wolf, giant, etc.

PROCEDURE:
1. Children can be seated at their desks, in front of you, or in almost any informal arrangement. Someone is selected to be *it* and is instructed to come up front, turn his back to the class, and close his eyes. Volunteers are picked, on the basis of someone who does not beg.

2. Select any animal or character desired, such as, the big bad wolf, Mickey Mouse, a witch, Santa Claus, the teacher, a kitty, and so on.

3. Have the rest of the class make a soft tapping sound on their desks or laps as the volunteer tiptoes up. This is to involve the whole class more completely, and to make it more difficult to detect where the footsteps are coming from.

4. When the actor is standing directly behind the person with his back turned, hold your hand up for the tapping to cease.

5. The child who has volunteered to perform now begins his *act*. First, he taps the waiting volunteer on the back, and that child, eyes still closed, says, "Who is it?" Now, the actor is to move and sound like the character or animal which was selected, disguising his voice. The waiting child tries to guess who it is. If, after two guesses, the actor succeeds in fooling the guesser, he *wins* and can either choose to be *it* or select someone else, and the game continues.

VARIATION A: A fun little verse to use is:
                 "Puddin' Tane, Puddin' Tane,
                 Ask me again and I'll tell you the same!"

VARIATION B: Have the actor turn and face the audience, performing for them as well as for the *guesser*.

VARIATION C: Have the actor move some distance away (sometimes even out the door). This requires "projection" of the voice and helps encourage children to find their stage voice.

EVALUATION: This game is a marvelous *ice breaker*, and enables many shy children to take a chance. The possibilities for role-playing and characterization are endless and non-threatening.

HANDS

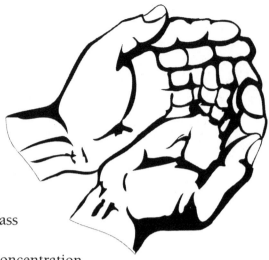

GRADES: K–8

TYPE OF ACTIVITY: Quiet, pantomime, full class

GOALS:
1. To develop focus and concentration

2. To become aware of the expressive use of our bodies, especially the hands

3. To provide a beginning, non-threatening pantomime activity

READINESS: Discuss and demonstrate *body language,* i.e., the way we sit, stand, hold our heads, tense our hands, or fidget. Show how our hands can speak for us, and illustrate that it is possible to communicate almost entirely with our hands, such as with the sign language used by the American Indians and the signing *speech* used by people who can't hear.

PROCEDURE:
1. Remind the children that we need to do this exercise in pantomime in order to focus.

2. Say, "Look at your hands. See what movements they can make. Pretend you are holding something sticky, soft, prickly, precious, hot, cold, etc."

3. Tell them they have a ball of clay and to *make* something.

4. Say, "Make your hands feel happy, sad, excited, frightened, proud, etc. Notice how it affects your body."

5. Say, "Pretend you have:

    a. a bird on your finger; he flies away; use your hands to coax him back;

    b. a crystal ball to tell the future;

    c. something 'magic' that keeps changing shape."

6. Say, "Open a box. Take something out."

EVALUATION: Marvelous! Easy and effective.

HISTORY — FAMOUS PEOPLE

GRADES: 3–8

TYPE OF ACTIVITY: Dramatization of historical figures related to curriculum study

GOALS:
1. To deepen understanding of the period of history being studied
2. To identify with the personality of historical figures
3. To motivate children to research and do creative writing
4. To offer an opportunity to dramatize

READINESS: Have a background discussion of the period of history being studied and some of the human problems which might have existed at that time. Talk about one's upbringing and how we are influenced by family, surroundings, economic conditions, health, etc.

PROCEDURE:
1. Explain that for this assignment they are to attempt to *be* the character chosen. Give examples: "I am Abraham Lincoln and I became very important in my lifetime…," "I am an Indian," and "I am a pioneer woman."
2. Put a list of possible choices on the board, asking for ideas from the class.
3. Give the class time to research their choice and instruct them to take notes.
4. As they begin their writing, look for good examples and read a portion to the class, trying to lead them away from too many dates and places and into personal aspects of their choice. (Some dates and locations are necessary, of course.)
5. Encourage art work, maps, costumes — *any* creative ideas they might wish to add to their project.

6. Share and critique, even selecting some to present to other classes.

7. Children should be prepared to answer questions about their character.

VARIATION A: Do in pairs, with dialogue.

VARIATION B: Do as an interview

VARIATION C: Do as a newscast with an *on the spot* reporter

SPECIAL NEEDS: Should this be too difficult an assignment for some, they could help with costuming, art work or do the interviewing.

EVALUATION: This is a wonderful way to personalize history and involve the children in a very exciting project. Sharing with another class provides extra motivation.

HISTORY — HEROES

GRADES: 1–8

TYPE OF ACTIVITY: Class activity involving individual work and small groups designed to bring history to life for children.

GOALS:
1. To provide heroes for children to identify with
2. To integrate art, music, and dance with curriculum drama
3. To give children an opportunity to act in serious roles
4. To deepen understanding of historical events

MATERIALS: Textbooks, songbooks, library books, supplementary material

READINESS: It is important for children to have real life heroes to identity with. Discussion could be had ahead of time as to what qualities produce a *hero*. Try to include concepts like honesty, integrity, courage, dignity.

PROCEDURE:
1. Selection of the hero or heroes can be made, either by the teacher or the class. Several possibilities are listed:

Example A: Special Day Heroes, such as: Abraham Lincoln, George Washington, Martin Luther King, and so forth. This would be a class project and enriched by countless available materials. Children can work individually, in groups or with a script. Encourage individual creativity.

Example B: Folk heroes, such as Davy Crocket, John Henry, Clementine, Casey Jones, Annie Oakley, and Buffalo Bill. All of these and many more are enriched with delightful dramatic songs which can be dramatized and preceded by little skits which the children create themselves.

Example C: General heroes such as the Suffragettes, the Temperance League, Civil War, American Revolution, native Americans and so forth. Songs and little skits greatly enrich these areas and bring people and history to life for children.

2. Research can be done on an individual basis as homework, or class time given so that material can be used from the library.

3. Small groups can work together planning creative ways of presentation.

4. (Optional) The focus can be a class project, involving *Actor/Audience* (page 3) as this subject makes an excellent performance piece.

EVALUATION: Children need heroes and really respond to altruistic ideals. The Martin Luther King presentation which is done every year by 6th graders at Middle School in Mill Valley is one of my most satisfying projects.

Reference Ideas:
   Heroes, Mark Brymer, grades 4-8
   I Remember Martin Luther King, Jr., Ruth Roberts, grades 6-8
   Johnny Appleseed, Jill Galling, grades 3-6
   Legend of the Twelve Moons, Ruth Roberts, grades 3-9
   My Country, John Wilson, grades 3-6
   Tall Tales and Heroes, Grace Hawthorne
   Folk Songs and Stones, John Wilson
   JW Pepper and Sons, 1-800-345-6296 for catalog

HISTORY — IMPROVISED THEMES

GRADES: 3–8

TYPE OF ACTIVITY: Improvisational acting activity done in groups

GOALS:
1. To involve children emotionally in historical events
2. To encourage critical thinking and problem solving ability
3. To help bring history to life and motivate children to learn more

READINESS: Have a group discussion relating to the historical material covered in class and try to have children relate to the feelings and problems involved. Explain that this will be group work and involve cooperation.

PROCEDURE:
1. Put the children in groups of 4 to 6 and either select a leader or let leadership evolve.
2. State the theme or let them think of their own as long as it relates to the curriculum.

   Examples: For early American history, imagine you are:
   a. A group of Indians discussing the advent of the white man.
   b. Explorers in the new land.
   c. Settlers moving west.
   d. Missionaries trying to establish missions.

   For later American history, imagine you are:
   a. Drawing up the first constitution.
   b. A group getting tired of foreign powers intervening (Boston Tea Party.)
   c. Debates over slavery and secession.
3. Give them time to plan but as this is to be improvisational, about 10 or 15 minutes should be sufficient.
4. Each group takes turns putting on its skit and in leading a discussion about what the students need to know.

EVALUATION: These are not to be polished skits but are fun to do and really do encourage children to find out more about their subject.

HISTORY — STUDENT SCRIPTS

GRADES: 3–8

TYPE OF ACTIVITY: Individual and small group writing and acting project related to class studies

GOALS:
1. To involve children actively in the study of history, improving their knowledge and understanding
2. To provide an opportunity for creativity, problem solving and leadership
3. To motivate children to write, act, and perform
4. To improve cooperative efforts with an emphasis on consideration

READINESS: Explain that this will be a project involving writing, research, and, ultimately acting. Have a discussion based on appropriate curriculum study. In some cases, relate to current issues so that children gradually come to understand that history gives us insight into the present and the future.

PROCEDURE:
1. Several beginning options are possible:
   a. Put subject ideas on the board, drawing from the students' suggestions.
   b. Pass out a sheet with prepared subject areas and allow them to chose.
   c. Have them make their own choice, also indicating whether they would like to work individually or in a group.
   d. Place them arbitrarily in a group, deliberately trying to break up cliques and emphasizing cooperation.
   e. Let them choose their own group.
2. Allow time for the planning and research stage.
3. Students need to share their ideas early on with helpful and considerate comments encouraged by the teacher.

4. Encourage facts to be incorporated into the skits and emphasize clarity of presentation (time, place, character's background, etc.)

5. Suggest art work, music, costumes, etc. but make it optional.

6. Final presentation will involve first their own class members, at which time it can be decided whether or not to arrange for a further audience.

VARIATION: Have children plan their skits with opposing viewpoints, such as those leading to the Civil War:

- North vs. South
- Indians vs. settlers
- Differing religious views
- Conflicts involving politics

EVALUATION: This is one of the best ways to involve the arts in the curriculum. The children identify and are motivated to be both academic and creative. I have found this assignment to be so motivational that students eagerly seek out information and have much better retention due to their involvement.

HOMONYMS

GRADES: 3–8

TYPE OF ACTIVITY: Speech and oral reading exercise. It can involve memorization, and be done as a solo, group, or choral work

GOALS:
1. To help with speech by correct enunciation and emphasis
2. To learn how the use of a word changes its meaning
3. To include *acting* with speaking
4. To learn homonyms
5. Excellent for group work, promoting cooperation with a specific focus

READINESS: Discuss first the meaning of the word *homonym* (a word that sounds the same but has a different spelling and meaning). give one example and then ask for ideas from the children, putting a list on the board.

PROCEDURE:

1. Choose one of the selections and put it on the board, or just do it orally.
2. Pass out papers with the list of homonym selections.
3. Ask the class to recite several choices in unison.
4. Ask for volunteers to do one alone with actions.
5. If desired, ask for more volunteers to come up and try to do in unison.

VARIATION A   Have each child try to memorize one and present it.

VARIATION B   Put the children in groups and ask them to be as creative as they wish in their manner of presentation.

EVALUATION: These little rhymes are marvelous for both individual and small group work. Children really learn to speak with proper emphasis for meaning. Each group seems to come up with a different and unique way of presenting its poem. This is an excellent exercise to promote better speech and confidence.

Sample selections:

I spent a *cent*
To buy some *scent*
And *sent* it to a friend, who wrote:
"This *vial* of stuff
Is *vile* enough
To use for making creosote.

She was *wrapped* up in a story...
The story held her *rapt*;
She read until her eyes were *red*.
Was she *wrapped*, or *rapt*, or trapped?

I can *sew* a seam,
And I can *sow* a seed.
So...
Wouldn't you know?
People call me a *sew* and *sow*!

Isn't that just *great*?
Something wrong with the *grate*!
No, something worse...
I just invited the wrong *guest*!
You *guessed* wrong.
You want a *loan*? Oh, leave me *alone*!

A sole is a fish one can eat,
And *soles* are the bottoms of your feet.
A *soul* we are told, is a spirit;
We cannot see it or hear it.
This would all be most amusing
If it weren't so confusing.

I stood on the *pier* to *peer* at the lake
A sign on a boat said, "For *Sale*."
So I went for *sail* and landed in jail.
Could it be that I made a mistake?

Which *one won?*
Number *Two.*
Too bad — I chose Number *One.*
Well, Number *Two* is now Number *One,*
Since he *won.*

If you *raise* a building
It goes up straight and tall;
If you *raze* a building,
No building's left at all!
Change a word a little bit,
And end up with the opposite.

Write your own:

all, awl; bale, bail; ball, bawl; beach, beech; blew, blue; breach, breech; bread, bred; buy, by, bye; capital, capitol; cede, seed; cite, sight, site; council, counsel; creak, creek; desert, dessert; discreet, discrete; feat, feet, fete; few, phew; flew, flue, flu; gnu, new; grate, great; hair, hare; hall, haul; heal, heel; hear, here; heard, herd; knead, need; lain, lane; lam, lamb; lie, lye; mail, male; mold, mould; one, won; pail, pale; pain, pane; pare, pear; peak, peek; peal, peel; pore, pour; principal, principle; rain, reign; right, write; ring, wring; rote, wrote; scene, seen; sea, see; seam, seem; stake, steak; strait, straight; tail, tale; their, there, they're; threw, through; to, too, two; toe, tow; vale, veil; ware, wear, where; weak, week; which, witch

HOW AND WHY STORIES

GRADES: 2–8

TYPE OF ACTIVITY: Writing and acting involving literature — whole class, individual, and small group work

MATERIALS: *Just So Stories* by Rudyard Kipling
Why the Sun and Moon Live in the Sky by Elphinstone Dayrell

GOALS:
1. To give students an awareness of the importance of questioning
2. To see common themes in other cultures
3. To have an opportunity to read and act out stories
4. To be stimulated to write their own stories, using much imagination

READINESS: Discuss the words *how* and *why* and the way all cultures have made up stories to explain things which were difficult to understand. Questioning is part of human nature, but impress on them the importance of learning to look for their own best answers.

PROCEDURE:
1. One successful method of approach is to read the selection first to them, encouraging note taking or drawing illustrations as the story is read. This aids recall ability, although some may prefer just to listen.

2. After the story has been read, call on children to tell it in their own words. Once a child exhibits enough confidence, suggest that he try to cast it. Naturally, there are many volunteers, and the whole procedure is stimulating and educational.

3. Have the children begin to improvise the acting, using the more confident story teller.

4. Appoint someone to take notes and help the story teller put together a simple script when he is finished. (This need not be detailed.)

5. A side activity which goes with these stories is to have the children write their own, as an in-class assignment, or for homework. It also makes a great assignment just to have them make a list of as many ideas as they can think of, or have the ideas called out, with the teacher putting the suggestions on the board.

Some examples are: How the Skunk got His Smell; Why the Porcupine Has Quills; Why the Bunny Has Long Ears; Why We Have Thunder and Lightning.

EVALUATION: These stories are ideal for dramatization. Children love playing animal or nature roles and make up remarkable stories of their own. These little playlets can make an excellent presentation for an audience.

INTRODUCTIONS

GRADES: K–8

TYPE OF ACTIVITY: Variety of methods to get acquainted and promote good feelings. Can be used as a memory exercise

GOALS:
1. To improve the art of communication
2. To promote class unity and good feelings
3. To learn everyone's name
4. To practice memorizing
5. To gain confidence with introductions

READINESS: Introduce, or re-introduce, yourself. Discuss how important it is to make eye contact when introducing yourself, and how many ways we can reacquaint ourselves with one another

PROCEDURE: *Intro Game A*

It's best to sit in a circle for this game so there can be eye contact. If the class is too large, make several circles. Start with yourself and give your name: "My name is Polly." Have the child on your right give his name, as well as yours: "My name is Mary, and this is Polly." The next child says his name, as well as the two previous ones: "My name is Joseph, this is Mary, and this is Polly," and so forth until the circle is completed. If someone has trouble or forgets, he may be assisted by anyone.

Intro Game B — Identification with Nature
Each child is told to think of an animal, a plant, a tree, an insect (or whatever), and either add that to his name or substitute his name, for example:

"I am Polly and I'm an eagle."
"I am Mary, and I'm a mouse. Polly is an eagle."

"I am Joseph, and I'm a tree. Mary is a mouse. Polly is an eagle," and so forth.

Or just:

"I am an eagle."

"I am a mouse. This is an eagle."

"I am a tree. She's a mouse. She's an eagle," etc.

VARIATION: Have a gesture, pose or movement go with your choice. This even works for plants, trees, rocks and the like. You can relate it to something being studied in class, thereby reinforcing your lesson.

Intro Game C — Adding Sound and Movement:

Each child gives a sound or a gesture in addition to his name or even as a substitution:

"I am Polly. Wheee!" (Throw hands up in delight.)

"I am Mary. Brrr!" (Shiver.) "This is Polly. Wheee!" (Throw hands up in delight.)

"I am Joe. Whew!" (Wipe brow.) "This is Mary. Brr!" (Shiver.) "This is Polly. Wheee!" (Throw hands up in delight), and so forth.

SPECIAL NEEDS: Shy or insecure children may have difficulty with these activities, but it is extremely important that they participate. Emphasize the positive, and allow leeway.

EVALUATION: Each grade level has different needs, so the approach can be appropriate to those needs. Introductions can be done any time to improve class tone, help with memory, or reinforce a curriculum subject.

INTRODUCTIONS EXERCISE

GRADES: 3–8

TYPE OF ACTIVITY: Small group involving whole class; quiet

GOALS:
1. To get acquainted
2. To practice making eye contact
3. To learn appropriate voice projection
4. To develop self-control

READINESS: Discuss use of eye contact and demonstrate the difference between looking at them and looking away while talking. Use different kinds of voices for introduction, and talk about response. Review consideration and how our attention needs to go towards the one speaking. Discuss *stage fright*. Share ideas about what causes it.

PROCEDURE:
1. Five or six children are called upon at a time and asked to stand in front of the class. Instruct them to stand up straight, with chins up, standing on both feet, with their hands behind their backs. This is their *first position*. It is one of dignity and security.

2. Ask them to take a small step forward, one at a time. Tell them that as each one does this, he should bring his hands out for possible use at this time, look at us, and say, "Hi!" give his name, and tell one thing about himself, i.e. what he doesn't like, where he lives, how many in his family, what pets he has, or whatever other simple thing he would like to share.

3. If comments are asked for at this time, the class should be cautioned to be considerate and make all comments positive, such as, "I liked Sam's voice." No comments should be allowed that single anyone out for embarrassment. It can be mentioned that later comments will be given that will have to do with ways we can all improve.

SPECIAL NEEDS: Use gentle encouragement, overlooking inadequate responses. Repeat this with smaller groups or even one to one for additional practice.

EVALUATION: A must! Well worth repeating. The benefits are invaluable as children gain confidence and security.

INTRODUCTION WITH AN OBJECT

GRADES: K–8

TYPE OF ACTIVITY: Short game to get better acquainted

MATERIALS:
Bag of peanuts *or*
Enough oranges for entire class *or*
Enough apples for entire class

GOALS:
1. To make introductions easier for children

2. To help gain appreciation of one another's differences

3. To provide a novel approach to conversation

READINESS: Getting acquainted can be difficult. Some children have an especially hard time. This could be discussed — or simply start right out with the game and have no prior explanation.

PROCEDURE:
1. Pass out fruit and nuts with instructions to take good care of it (not to eat it).

2. Have children observe item and notice what is special about it.

3. Have children name their objects.

4. Ask children to introduce their object to another child's object.

5. Children should tell what is special about their object.

6. Ask children whose objects were introduced to introduce themselves to objects of another pair.

7. Children may eat or save their objects.

EVALUATION: Excellent activity for a group — a real *ice-breaker.* I have even experienced this little game as an adult and found it a great way to get acquainted.

I'VE LOST MY SHEEP

GRADES: K–3

TYPE OF ACTIVITY: Circle game, quiet, little movement

GOALS:
1. Quiet game to help settle and focus
2. To improve class tone and help shy ones express themselves
3. To build self-image for children
4. To improve observation ability

READINESS: Talk about the importance of observing things carefully, *attention* being the real key to intelligence. Tell the children that this game will help give them practice in noting details about each other.

PROCEDURE:
1. Have the children make a circle. (This can also be done with children sitting in front of you.)
2. Demonstrate how the game is played by walking around the circle and saying something like:
   - "I'm looking for my sheep… It has blue eyes, is very friendly, a black and white striped shirt, a nice voice, is considerate, has brown hair…, etc.
   - At this point, or whenever someone has figured out who it is and calls out the correct name, that person takes the teacher's place.
3. Remind the *searcher* to try not to look too often at his *sheep.*
4. Two or more children can be selected to sit in the middle and try to figure out who the sheep is, rather than having it called out by someone in the circle; then it becomes a contest to see who figures out the *sheep* first, and the winner becomes *it.*

SPECIAL NEEDS: Use this game to give confidence to children with special needs by making up complimentary and supportive comments about them.

EVALUATION: This game is fun and gives an opportunity to build confidence and ego. Even older children love it!

JINGLES

GRADES: 2–6

TYPE OF ACTIVITY: Small group with emphasis on speech

GOALS:
1. To help with enunciation
2. To provide a small group activity using cooperation
3. To give an opportunity for a creative writing assignment
4. To have a non-threatening opportunity for children to perform

READINESS: Define and discuss *enunciation* (clear and definite pronunciation.) Ask why this is important. Demonstrate speaking both ways.

PROCEDURE:
1. Select a jingle and put on the board. In addition to the following easy and effective jingles, there are many, many more short poems (see *Tongue Twisters*, page 150) which could be used:

   I blow bubbles
   Big, big bubbles
   Bright bubbles
   Blue bubbles
   Bright, blue bubbles

   Pitter, patter
   Pitter, patter
   Raindrops patter down
   Pitter, patter
   Pitter, patter
   Over mountain,
   Field and town

   Merrily, merrily
   All the spring,
   Merrily, merrily
   Small birds sing.

All through April
All through May
Small birds merrily
Sing all day.

Hu is a huffy breath
Hu is a blow
Hear how I Huff it
Ho, high, ho

2. Recite the jingle, all together, several times.

3. Call on a volunteer to come up and recite the jingle.

4. Ask him to do it again with gestures, even saying to him, "Try overdoing it! Be dramatic!"

5. Ask for more volunteers and request that they attempt to do the jingle together (with gestures.) Build the chorus to as many as seem effective.

6. Optional: Request the students to write their own, either singly or in pairs, and add to your list of choices.

EVALUATION: One of the main benefits of this approach in regard to speech is that it requires a slowing down and separation of words and phrases and emphasis given to important key words. This comes naturally when it is required that they try to do it together. It therefore has the desired effect of allowing the students to have more confidence and better delivery when they do individual recitations.

KEEPING YOUR COOL

GRADES: 2–6

TYPE OF ACTIVITY: Done in group or pairs to improve concentration level

GOALS:
1. To improve concentration
2. To help children learn to keep control of themselves
3. To encourage good posture
4. To help children relate better to one another

READINESS: Impress on the children what a marvelous ability it is to be *in charge* of yourself, and not subject to react inappropriately, or to be subject to distraction or embarrassment. Discuss situations where this ability would be particularly useful. Draw from their experience and ideas.

PROCEDURE:
1. Groups of children take turns coming up in front, standing in First Position, hands behind the back, looking straight ahead, and attempting not to change their expressions. First try to distract them yourself, and one by one, as they *lose their cool*, they must sit down. After a time, ask a few *clowns* to help until there is a winner.

2. Pairs are selected on a random basis, but children are cautioned that they will be exchanging partners and are not to react to any such changes. First, they sit facing one another, about one foot apart.

   • **Step One:** The children close their eyes and attempt to sit motionless. Go around and straighten heads, shoulders and backs, and separate hands, as posture is important for this exercise. Once they are able to sit still in this position for a minute or two without giggling or moving, allow them to open their eyes.

- **Step Two:** They attempt to look directly into the other person's eyes without changing expression or *cracking up.*

- **Step Three:** Children take turns being pupil and teacher. The pupil tries to maintain the composure of **Steps One and Two, while the teacher** tries to distract. The *teacher* is not to come closer than six inches, but may literally say or do anything. If the *pupil* loses his composure, th*e teacher* says "Flunk!" and repeats the same action until the *student* is able to keep his *cool.* After a time, the roles are reversed. Many students may not be able to do this and they should return to Steps One and Two again until they feel more secure. They are to keep trying over and over until success is achieved, but sometimes the combination is a poor one and I make a switch in order to better insure *success.*

EVALUATION: The group exercise is a favorite at any age. The children request it over and over, and it really does have a beneficial effect. The exercise in pairs works best with children from 2nd grade on up. It is more personal and an ideal way to match up pairs for better feelings.

LIGHTHOUSE GAME

GRADES: K–3

TYPE OF ACTIVITY: Quiet, mostly stationary game. Emphasizes sense of hearing. Requires large empty space.

GOALS:

1. To promote cooperation of the group

2. To hold a *freeze*

3. To help with the imagination and involve shy children

4. To learn to identify where a sound is coming from

READINESS: Discuss the sense of hearing and how we can train it with careful attention. Remind them, or play again, the *Listening Game* (see page 73) and point out how special this sense is.

PROCEDURE:

1. Find a large empty space

2. Select one child to be the lighthouse, and another to be the tugboat.

3. All the other children are told that they are rocks, and must not move. Ask the rocks to spread out and leave space between.

4. Blindfold the tugboat, *because it is very foggy*. He must then try to find the lighthouse by going towards the sound being made by the lighthouse — "WhooGaa," or any such appropriate sound. Of course, the little boat must be *very careful* not to bump the rocks, so it must go slowly and gently. Small children love this game.

5. Instruct the rocks to make soft "swish, swish" sounds, to imitate the sound of lapping water.

6. The game ends when the tugboat gets safely to the lighthouse, and new people are chosen to be tugboat and lighthouse.

SPECIAL NEEDS: This game demonstrates in a small degree what it might be like to be blind and how the blind must develop their sense of hearing, as well as their other senses.

EVALUATION: Small children love this game, and want to repeat it over and over. It has a calming effect on the group.

LISTENING

GRADES: K–3

TYPE OF ACTIVITY: Quiet, to emphasize sense of hearing

GOALS:
1. To calm and quiet children
2. To emphasize our sense of hearing
3. To identify *problem* children and demonstrate the need for co-operation

READINESS: Discuss our senses and how they can be trained to do a much better job for us. Emphasize that this exercise will need everyone's cooperation. "A chain is only as strong as its weakest link" is a saying that fits for this concept.

PROCEDURE:
1. Make sure that everyone is seated comfortably where they are not touching anyone.

2. Say, "We are all going to try to be completely quiet, and notice what we can hear. Close your eyes and listen."

3. After one or two minutes, ask them to open their eyes and share what they heard. (If someone makes noise before then, the exercise stops at that point.)

4. Encourage the children to share something *different* and not the same as has already been shared, and to share things that they really heard, not imagined.

VARIATION A: Have a collection of sounds for the children to listen to, either on tape or a variety of musical instruments, bells, blocks to clack, etc. The children can close their eyes and try to identify.

VARIATION B: Children take turns being blindfolded or turning their backs, while individuals are selected from the class to make sounds using objects provided.

EVALUATION: This activity has a marvelous calming effect. It can also be made a homework assignment for them to take a little time, sit all by themselves, and *listen* to all the sounds they can hear. Homework could also be to bring in sound making devices or even make a tape to bring into class.

LITERATURE — GREAT BOOKS

GRADES: 3–8

TYPE OF ACTIVITY: Dramatic or musical presentations using one of the great books of literature.

GOALS:
1. To stimulate children to read an outstanding work of literature and to personalize and internalize the drama and concepts involved

2. To include music and drama in the presentation, thereby giving all the children in class the benefits derived from such participation

3. To provide an opportunity for vocabulary enrichment, grammar, punctuation, spelling, and any creative tie-in the classroom teacher wishes to make

4. To stimulate creativity, cooperation, and outside research by small group work

5. To encourage individual special talents

6. To involve community and parents and consequently produce positive feelings and added support for the school

READINESS: First have the children read and discuss the book. This can be done in segments, developing a script as you go along — or read the book first and have some in-depth discussions before starting with your play (see examples). If possible have the music teach songs related to the script (see examples).

PROCEDURE:
1. Build your script either from the book itself, using the exact wording of the author and picking key sections to dramatize, or have the children develop their own script from the *telling* of the story.

2. Pick your story tellers. They will be key to the success of the production so will need to have confidence and voices that carry well.

3. *Try outs* (page 53) for particular parts should be done primarily on a basis of their choice. Motivation is the *key* and the desire to do a part will go a long way towards its successful execution.

4. Parts which are very popular can be chosen any number of ways:

   - Teacher selection based on responsibility and aptitude.
   - Pantomime situations and "bring to life" for improvisational skills.
   - Ask that the children read or attempt to memorize a few lines and deliver them.
   - Make it optional homework for them to practice a section outside of school hours.

5. Select parts by whichever means seem appropriate for a particular class.

6. Start with rehearsals. Some of the time, work with them individually, and some of the time, have an audience of their peers give them helpful critique: "How could this be better? — clearer? — more enjoyable?" Criticism is usually considerate and helpful, and children really respond to one another's suggestions.

   - "I would like it better if it was louder."
   - "Some parts got a little rushed."
   - "When you look at us, we feel involved."
   - "Try a little drama and action to give interest and emphasis."
   - "Give us a little time to think after each sentence."
   - "Boy, that was terrific!"

   Children love giving compliments to each other, and it improves class tone.

7. See that each child does the best job possible. In some cases, it may be found that a student does not feel comfortable as a story teller, or does not have the skill for a particular part and it can be mutually decided that another part would be more comfortable.

Example A: Treasure Island

   This was an exceptionally successful production done by a 5th grade class with the added help of their music teacher. We used 10 story tellers. The actors pantomimed when the story teller spoke and *came to life* with appropriate dialogue when they stopped. The entire class was involved with the music and singing and everyone spoke of the production and their involvement in it as unforgettable.

Example B: Tom Sawyer (4th or 5th grade)

We developed this play by first having the children read the book and then develop their script. We asked them to copy out what they considered key sections and put together our script. We used music from a play, parts were selected and rehearsals began. This production was superb and not difficult in terms of memorization. Only the story tellers had to memorize word for word and some were allowed to have note cards.

Example C: James and the Giant Peach (3rd grade)

The procedure used for the development of this play was delightful. Each week several children took turns *telling the story*. When we found a gifted story teller (there were many), we asked that the students jot down notes for themselves so they could recapture their part of the story. Therefore, the script was truly done by the students themselves and consequently was so fresh and delightful that it made the play exceptionally entertaining. We listed all the many roles possible on the board, even including such things as *sea gulls* and *city people*. They were asked to put down both their first and second choice. Many did not want major roles and where there were many requests for the same role, we had try outs and decisions were easily made without hurt feelings. The children made their own costumes, and sets. The show was marvelous!

EVALUATION: This technique can be used for any of the great books. The involvement of the children deepens their appreciation and understanding of literature. Creativity engenders enthusiasm.

MACHINE

GRADES: 2–8

TYPE OF ACTIVITY: Group activity to further coop-erative feelings

GOALS:
1. To promote cooperation and positive group feelings
2. To develop and make use of the intuitive
3. To greater perfect the *freeze*
4. To impress on children the power of concentration

READINESS: There are several different ways to begin this activity. One of the best ways is to have the children move around with their panto-mime exercises, paying particular attention to the *Freeze,* pointing out that it requires much energy to do a really good *Freeze.* Noth-ing should distract them. Walk by, make faces, even clap your hands, and in this way select six to ten students who are able to maintain their *Freeze.* Selection may also be made simply by asking for vol-unteers.

PROCEDURE:
1. Those selected to create *The Machine* are first required to stand in First Position (straight, with dignity). Remind them that they are not to look at you, but to look straight ahead, with their eyes fixed on some object in the distance. Point out, when this feat is accomplished by all participants, that they now have sufficient concentration to create their machine.

2. One child is selected to take a step forward and ask that some-one in the audience give them a suggestion. The child is di-rected to say very firmly, "Machine, please," and then repeat the machine given by saying, "A washing machine (or whatever). Thank you." Just for fun, tell them to ask for a nonsense ma-chine, which can either be a made up word or something non-existent, like *a machine to do your homework.*

3. Once the particular machine is selected, the child who has requested the suggestion is instructed to take a position and *Freeze*. It can be any position, but really stress the perfect *Freeze* as being of the utmost importance. The next instructions are for the rest of the children to join, actually making contact with someone, as the idea is to become part of the group and to *Freeze*. If it is a class with peers for audience, ask that they note the children with the best *Freezes*, for they will be the ones to make it work.

4. Then say, "When I turn this machine on the first time, it will not make a sound, but move in *pantomime*." This is stressed, because it helps with their concentration. When you reach over, pretending there is a switch in front, and say, "Click!" they will consistently move in amazingly synchronized movements. When you say, "Click!" again to turn the *Machine* off, they will stop simultaneously.

5. The second time you do it say, "And now, the machine will make a sound, if it is the type of machine that is supposed to make a sound. Some parts may remain silent and motionless, as always on any machine." Then say, "Click!" again, and the *machine* makes appropriate sounds. The volume can be turned up or down, and the *machine* may be speeded up or slowed down. The children are also instructed to hold their last Freeze until the audience has finished clapping. Choose a new group, and the same procedure is used. Try to let all the children in the class participate as part of the *machine* in this exercise.

VARIATION: Once the machine has been made by the group, ask them to spread out and individually become the same machine. They will do this with no questions or hesitation. Once they have a freeze — turn them off and on and add sound as you did with the group.

EVALUATION: This is perhaps one of the most impressive and beneficial of all the exercises. It can be used as a performance piece to entertain an audience, or simply for practice and fun. Children of all ages love it, and never tire of doing it.

MATH — DRAMATIC APPROACHES FOR PRIMARY

GRADES: K–3

TYPE OF ACTIVITY: Variety of tangible and dramatic approaches to augment math concepts and skills

GOALS:
1. To involve children with some visible and tangible means of learning math concepts
2. To make learning fun by the use of games
3. To stimulate the intuitive and problem solving abilities innate in children

READINESS: Children of any age often find math to be very threatening. Any reassurance or sharing of personal experience is helpful. Let them know that math can be exciting and fun. It is vitally important that good solid foundational skills be built at this time.

PROCEDURE: The following are some helpful ideas and suggestions for dramatic games and activities.

1. Cuisinnaire rods (rods which show size as related to number — available at any teacher's store), blocks of different shapes, objects to represent size and weight for the *What Is It?* game (page 163).

2. *Concentration Game* — use any of the tables to reinforce computational skills (page 9).

3. Whole Group pantomime — Have children improvise their response to words like addition, subtraction, pyramid, rectangle, fraction, weight, relationship (anything the teacher feels appropriate). Split into *Audience/Actor* (page 3).

4. Small group planning — Put children in groups of 3 or 4 and ask that they come up with word problems. They can *write* them out, *act* them out, or both.

5. Round the World game — One child starts by standing next to

another who is seated. Flash cards are used or a verbal problem is given and the first child to respond moves on to the next. If the child seated responds first, that child stands and goes on to the next. It can be decided how many places a child need move to win the game.

6. *Direction Taking* (page 17)

7. Ask the children to bring in math games or make them up

EVALUATION: The more involved children get, the better they learn. Healthy competition stimulates sportsmanship and confidence.

MATH — DRAMATIC APPROACHES FOR SECONDARY

GRADES: 4–8

TYPE OF ACTIVITY: Group and individual activities designed to use children's intuitive and creative abilities

GOALS:
1. To help develop children's problem solving abilities
2. To deepen conceptual learning
3. To improve computational and analytical math skills
4. To have fun by using games for learning

READINESS: Discuss the many ways we use math in real life and how seeing patterns in math relates to other types of learning, even music and art. Discuss personal experiences students have had (both good and bad) regarding math. Share some yourself if possible.

PROCEDURE: The following are some games and activities which involve the whole body approach:

1. *Concentration* game (page 9), to reinforce percents, fractions, formulas or any concept.

2. Group pantomime. Have children demonstrate with their bodies; horizontal, vertical, intersection, north, south, acute angle, circumference, volume. Make a list, have the children add to it.

3. *Wordo* (page 167) uses math terms. Have them *show* as well as *tell* the meaning.

4. *Direction Taking* (page 17) is a marvelous activity to improve concentration and skills.

5. Have students compose and act out word problems.

6. Have children work in pairs or small groups and ask that they think of ways to *demonstrate* concepts, formulas, theorems, equa-

tions, *whatever*! Their creativity and ingenuity are boundless. Emphasize clarity and tangible, visual approaches.

7. Ask the class to come in with games and activities for making math come alive. Have a corner of the room available for these things.

8. *Round the World* (see Primary Math #5). Make questions suitable to capability.

EVALUATION: Math proficiency helps children gain confidence. Problem solving, experimentation, and a variety of approaches really adds another dimension, using *both* sides of the brain, so that both the analytical and creative aspects of one's learning power are used.

MEMORY GAME

GRADES: K–8

TYPE OF ACTIVITY: Quiet; involving use of senses and development of memory

MATERIALS: Those appropriate for the lesson. Paper and pencil

GOALS:
1. To help improve memory
2. To relate the senses to memory
3. To have fun where children can see their own improvement

READINESS: The art of memorization is a skill, like any other, and can be improved upon with practice. Some children have a natural ability to memorize easily, but for others, it is much more difficult. I will share personal experience such as looking up a phone number 100 times and then decide to find a way to fix the number in my mind. Emphasize that any of the senses can be used effectively to memorize.

PROCEDURE:
1. Put a number of objects on a tray or table.

2. Children walk around the display, either as a group or in pairs.

3. Cover the objects so they cannot be seen and then ask that the children write down as many as they can remember.

    a. If working in pairs, one can dictate to the other
    b. If children are unable to write or spell, they can draw pictures and then identify

VARIATION A: Use objects which are especially suited to the sense of touch, such as cotton batting, a marble, something bristly, an eraser, etc. The children can either be blindfolded or told to use both sight and touch to remember.

VARIATION B: Select objects with a distinctive smell or taste and ask that the children use these senses to help remember. If a blindfold is used, pairs work well.

VARIATION C: Have objects on the tray related to what is being studied in class: leaves, rocks, measurement devices, etc.

SPECIAL NEEDS: There will be a notable difference in ability so try to have each child compete with himself, rather than each other.

EVALUATION: This game can be used again and again in a great variety of ways. It can easily be related to almost any area of the curriculum so children have fun and learn at the same time.

MIRROR

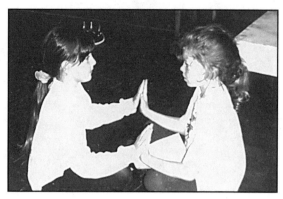

GRADES: K–8

TYPE OF ACTIVITY: Easy and fun for any age. Improves concentration

GOALS:
1. To develop powers of observation
2. To develop powers of concentration
3. To improve class feelings by being a good mixer

READINESS: Demonstrate with a mirror how the reflection is the opposite, but exact. Discuss how carefully we are going to try to pattern ourselves after our partner. Pass around mirrors if there is time. Have them make faces, say sounds and words clearly: click, fun, pretty, "b," "m," "sh" etc. This can be phonetic and enunciation practice too, as part of the game.

PROCEDURE:
1. Tell children to select a partner, or give them one. If you do the selecting, remind them first never to hurt anyone's feelings by acting as though they don't want them for a partner. In any case, it is a good idea to keep switching partners so they become accustomed to being with other children.

2. Each pair can again decide who is to be number one and who will be number two. One child will be the mirror while the other initiates the expression, or you can simply say, "Copy one another. Do not touch, but mirror each other's expressions."

3. Ask them to keep their motions simple and slow, using only their faces and heads first, and then their hands, and finally their whole bodies.

4. Later instruct that one should *follow* the other moving around the floor.

5. Look for pairs who are concentrating well, and occasionally direct the other children to stop their activities and look at a particular pair. If time permits, each pair will be observed by the others.

EVALUATION: This is a wonderful exercise which can be used again and again with children of all ages. They never tire of it, and learn a great deal. It is an excellent *mixer*, so children get used to one another, thereby promoting good feelings. It is also an excellent way to improve speech where children learn by observing and have fun doing it!

MUSICAL DRAMA

GRADES: K–8

TYPE OF ACTIVITY: Active and creative, involving entire class

MATERIALS: Recorded music or piano

GOALS:
1. To stimulate the creative, intuitive side of the brain
2. To become aware of the relationship of movement and music
3. To encourage freedom of expression

READINESS: Discuss how music inspires us in a variety of ways. Use the piano or recorded music to demonstrate (fast, slow, light, heavy, sad, happy, marching, etc.) Point out how music is tied to history, culture, and heritage.

PROCEDURE:
1. If piano is used, simply tell the children to do what the music *tells* them to do: high, low, fast, slow, heavy, light, skip, dance, etc. Side coach if appropriate.
2. If recorded music is used, tell them to move the way it makes them feel.
3. When the music stops, have the children *Freeze*.
4. (Optional) Choose a leader for the group to follow or put in small groups and appoint leaders for each group.

VARIATION A: Draw pictures and make up stories inspired by the music.

VARIATION B: Ask for a volunteer to improvise a story which the children act out. (Turn the music low or off as the story teller speaks.)

EVALUATION: A creative activity, full of surprises, and suitable for impromptu performances. It is especially good for promoting individual creativity.

NEWS BROADCAST

GRADES: 4–8

TYPE OF ACTIVITY: Class activity designed to keep students abreast of current news, improve communication skills, evaluations, and group work

TIME: This is an ongoing activity that takes one to two hours of teacher preparation time, but once the materials have been made, they can be used indefinitely, from week to week and even year to year

MATERIALS: Cardboard (large and smaller pieces), laminated weather map

GOALS:
1. To give children a greater knowledge and appreciation of the world around them

2. To improve all speaking skills

3. To make specific evaluations designed to improve communication and critiquing skills

4. To stress the importance of teamwork for success of a project

5. To have fun with an ongoing learning activity

READINESS: Discuss the importance of current events and ask how many watch the news. There can also be a discussion of democracy vs. totalitarianism or other repressive societies where much news is withheld. There can be an awareness that our news is also often controlled to a certain extent. Ask open ended questions.

- "Why and how would this happen?"
- "What did they do before TV, radio, or newsprint?"

PROCEDURE: 1. Make a chart out of cardboard (See Illustration #1), and have a space for each area of news you wish to cover, having each section contain a pocket in which you can insert a 3 x 5 inch index card with the student's name, date and role. This makes it simple to keep track of student rotation as they take on a different role.

There can be two or more class groups which are responsible for the news production every week on a designated day.

2. Students are instructed to make notes on index cards and to practice in front of a mirror and/or with another person to help with the critique prior to the class broadcast.

3. Each group can decide on a name, and create a backdrop. They should also have a large, laminated weather map, 3 x 12 inch tagboard cards with the name of each role which is to be put in front of each newscaster, and large, clear prompter cards to be used by the floor manager, listing some do's and don'ts, such as:

Speak louder	Slow down
Look at camera	Stop looking at notes
Sit up straight	Good information
Nice presence	Stop fidgeting
Smile	Showing improvement

These cards can be made up ahead of time by the teacher, or each group or Floor Manager can determine what they want to use. The Floor Manager holds up the appropriate prompter cards during the newscast.

4. An evaluation card (see Illustration #2) is easily filled in by the teacher as each child does the newscast. Initially, class time can be allowed for some in-depth critiquing. Students can keep their grade sheets in a folder so they can note their improvement.

5. Optional — Newscasts can be videotaped from time to time and evaluations made on oral presentations.

EVALUATION: This is a wonderful ongoing project and once the materials have been made it can be used in a variety of ways. Children can keep abreast of current events, as well as approach history as though it were occurring in the *here and now*. Anytime current happenings or history can be personalized and in some way dramatized, children internalize, remember and are motivated to find out *more* about the subject!

Illustration #1

NEWSCAST
TEAM

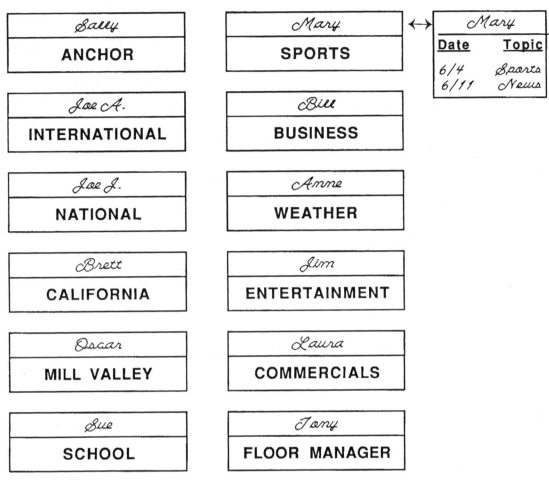

Sally		*Mary*	
ANCHOR		**SPORTS**	

Mary	
Date	**Topic**
6/4	*Sports*
6/11	*News*

Joe A.
INTERNATIONAL

Bill
BUSINESS

Joe J.
NATIONAL

Anne
WEATHER

Brett
CALIFORNIA

Jim
ENTERTAINMENT

Oscar
MILL VALLEY

Laura
COMMERCIALS

Sue
SCHOOL

Tony
FLOOR MANAGER

Illustration #2

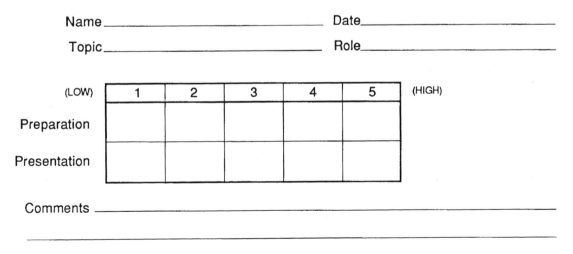

CURRENT EVENTS GRADE SHEET

Name_____ Date_____

Topic_____ Role_____

(LOW)	1	2	3	4	5	(HIGH)
Preparation						
Presentation						

Comments _____

OBJECTS

GRADES: K–8

TYPE OF ACTIVITY: Whole group pantomime

MATERIALS: Demonstration of objects optional. None necessary

GOALS:
1. To increase the ability to concentrate and focus
2. To decrease self-consciousness
3. To provide a creative way for children to express themselves

READINESS: Have a few objects available. Handle them. Pass them around and ask that the children pantomime holding or using the object when they don't have it. Discuss how we use this ability in drama.

PROCEDURE:
1. The following list gives some useful ideas:

    a axe, apple, arrow, auto, ant

    b ball, bat, butterfly, bag, book, blanket, bird, bottle, box, bowling ball, blocks

    c candy, chair, chicken, camera, cat

    d dog, door, duck, drum, doll, dish, discus, drawer

    e egg

    f flashlight, fan, feather, folding chair, favorite toy, flower

    g grease, glass, glue, game

    h hammer, hats, hose, helmet

    i ice cream cone, ice, ice skates, ink

    j jacks, jelly, jar, jack-in-the-box, junk

    k kite, knife, kitten, kaleidoscope, key

    l lemon, light, lamb, ladybug, lapdog, lock, licorice

    m match, mirror, magic ball, mud, mixer

    n newspaper, nickel, needle, nut

p pole, package, pencil, present, pie, paint brush, picture, pitcher

r robot, rope, razor, rug, ribbon

s stick, string, saw, shovel, slug, shoes (old, new), socks

t truck, toy, tire, tie

u umbrella

v vase, vest, violin, volleyball

w window, worm, wind-up toy, walking stick, whip

x xylophone

y yo yo

z zoo

VARIATION A:	Add ideas as to what to do with object, i.e., *open* window; get kite *stuck* in tree, *try on* hats, etc.
VARIATION B:	Ask them to *be* the object
VARIATION C:	Use Audience/Actor and ask for comments (This sharpens observation abilities.)
VARIATION D:	Call out letters of the alphabet and have the children think of their own objects beginning with that letter.

EVALUATION: Great activity for all; sharpens awareness

OUR SOLAR SYSTEM

GRADES: K–3

TYPE OF ACTIVITY: Large group, involving movement related to astronomy

MATERIALS: Large room/empty space
Optional: charts, drawing paper, objects for demonstration

GOALS:
1. To internalize an understanding of our solar system
2. To provide a meaningful follow-up to discussion of heavens
3. To stimulate curiosity and make learning enjoyable

READINESS: Using charts and real objects, show and demonstrate the rotation of the earth, orbits for planets, earth, sun, etc.

PROCEDURE:
1. Demonstrate *rotate,* and have all children rotate
2. Demonstrate *orbit* around another object or child. Have the child rotate while you orbit, then reverse.
3. Have all children work in pairs, experimenting with *rotate* and *orbit.*
4. Give each child a role: sun, earth, planets, moon, asteroid, and show them how they are to orbit around appropriately (earth around the sun, planets around the sun, moons around the earth, asteroids around the planets, etc.).
5. Show by charts or objects relative size and distance.
6. Let the children change roles.

EVALUATION: This is both fun and meaningful, and it helps internalize some of the concepts. Even kindergartners have been able to do this exercise for an audience of parents.

PEOPLE

GRADES: K–8

TYPE OF ACTIVITY: Group pantomime; bring to life

GOALS:
1. Internalization of concentration
2. Better understanding of others
3. Opportunity to fantasize and characterize

READINESS: Children love to play different roles and do so as soon as they have even rudimentary speech. This activity is ideal as an outlet for that need. There could be a discussion first as to possible occupations *when they grow up*. It gives a teacher opportunity for insight into a child's imagination and to give dignity and importance to all occupations, based on integrity and enjoyment of life.

PROCEDURE: The following list gives some useful ideas:
- a actor, artist, athlete, acrobat, architect
- b balloon salesman, banker, baseball player, beggar, barber, boxer, beautician, butler, bellhop, bricklayer, baker
- c circus clown, cook, caretaker, conductor, checker, carpenter, courtesan (older), clerk, cowboy
- d dancer, doctor, drummer, draftsman
- e engineer, entertainer, elf, electrician
- f father, football player, firemen, forester, fortune teller, factory worker, farmer, fashion designer
- g giant, geologist, grocer, gardener, gymnast, gentleman
- h haberdasher, hockey player
- i inventor
- j jeweler, jockey, judge
- k king
- l launderer, lecturer, lion tamer

m mother, machinist, magician, mechanic, merchant

n nurse, nursery school teacher

o opera star

p policeman, politician, president, poet, priest, painter, pianist, pilot, prize-fighter, principal

q queen

r rich man, ringmaster, rock star, repairman

s salesman (shoe/car/clothes, etc.), singer, small child, sculptor, scientist, soldier

t teacher, teenager, thief, tightrope walker, truck driver, trainman, taxi driver

v violinist, veterinarian

w waiter, wrestler, writer, weatherman, watchman, window washer, weight lifter

z zookeeper

1. Call out types of people; have children pantomime; remind them not to look at each other while performing.

2. Give each character something to *do*, or a place to *be*, i.e., window washer drops bucket, salesman trying to sell something, magician doing tricks, etc.

3. *Close eyes, picture what or who you'd like to be; come to life.*

4. Tell them they can be anyone they like in a story, book, or movie.

| VARIATION A: | Divide class into Audience/Actor and have audience guess *who* they are. |
| VARIATION B: | Have them look for pictures in magazines and make scrapbook and write stories. |

SPECIAL NEEDS: This is a very therapeutic exercise for all, and often gives the teacher insight into characteristics and problems which a child may have.

EVALUATION: Fun and good training for all ages.

PLACES

GRADES: K–4

TYPE OF ACTIVITY: Full class, pantomime, bring to life

MATERIALS: None necessary; pictures optional

GOALS:
1. To improve concentration abilities
2. To provide an introduction to *experiencing* and using the imagination
3. To develop creativity and originality

READINESS: Discuss, or possibly show pictures of places and how they differ and what we might do in those places. Ask for ideas and add them to list.

PROCEDURE:
1. Call out different places for the children to experience, allowing 20-30 seconds for them to experience each place. Some handy ideas are:

   a air

   b beach, baseball game, basketball game (watching), birthday party

   c carnival, circus, carousel, celebration, catastrophe, car race

   d crowded department store, desert, Disneyland, at desk

   f football game, farm, freeway, fountain

   g game, (watching), garden, grocery store, gym

   h home, haystack

   j jury, jungle, juvenile hall, jeep, jet

   k kitchen,

   l lake, pile of leaves, living room

   m movie, mountain, museum, magic show, masquerade, mud

o   ocean, orchestra, opera

p   park, ping pong game, playground, play (performance), party

s   swimming pool, store, school, ship, swamp

t   train, toy store, tar pit, throne, tower, track, train

v   in a vacuum, vessel, village

w   wagon, war, water, web, wigwam

y   yacht

z   zoo

2. Give them something to *do* in each place, or add a weather situation

VARIATION A:	Ask children to *lie down flat*, or stand and close their eyes and imagine: a place you'd like to be; a place you don't like; a magic place; a place you've dreamed about. Tell them that they are in that place on a given signal.
VARIATION B:	Tell them to concentrate on a certain *place* in a story, book, or movie. Come to life and pantomime being in that place.
VARIATION C:	Divide into Audience/Actor. Take turns guessing where they are. This can be done in small groups also.
VARIATION D:	Toy Shop: Have children think of some toy in a toy shop and freeze like that toy. Then come to life at a certain signal.

SPECIAL NEEDS: Great for all, especially for children with special needs.

EVALUATION: Wonderful fun and wonderful training. This list is handy for a variety of purposes.

POETRY —
DRAMATIC POEMS

GRADES: K–4

TYPE OF ACTIVITY: Group lesson involving memorization, recitation, and composition

GOALS:

1. To help children learn to recite

2. To help with memorization techniques

3. To promote imagery, rhythm, and meaning

4. To provide practice for speech training and enunciation

READINESS: Poetry is a delightful and natural means of expression for children. They readily memorize and compose. My feeling is that it can be used to enrich understanding and retention of many subjects.

PROCEDURE:

1. The poem is read aloud to the class with as much feeling and clarity as possible.

2. Discuss the meaning of the poem, first overall and then stanza by stanza, emphasizing words that give imagery and explaining words that need to be better understood. Care should be taken not to over-analyze the poem, but mainly to answer questions which might come from the children.

3. If each child has a copy, the poem can be read in unison with the teacher clearly providing the leadership.

4. For some lines and stanzas ask them not to lOOK but to *listen*. Say a section with the proper emphasis, then ask them to repeat.

5. Ask them to stand and add a gesture or two for emphasis if at all possible.

6. It can be helpful to make a chart, listing a number of poems which have been studied. That way you can ask which one they'd like to work on, and gradually they come to know several by heart.

7. Encourage children to write their own poetry. Drama can be used to augment the writing the children have done. They can work on their oral expression and experiment in various ways for the dramatization of the poem. Sometimes it will involve the whole class, and the author can either read it or select someone with a stronger voice.

Example A: Make the subject *emotions* and have children pantomime.

LOVE

Love is a floating cloud
Every time you reach out to touch it,
It jumps away.
I play tag with Love
I am always it.

Sarah Madland, Grade 5

ANGER

Anger flies through the air munching
snacking on all living things.
It has devils and fire,
melted dolls and toys,
where demon growls
and werewolves burn.

Greg A., Grade 5

Example B: Kindergarten and primary grades can recite and act out any of the nursery rhymes.

Example C: Use Shel Silverstein's books and have children work in small groups, pairs or individually to plan creative presentations.

Example D: Use any one of countless poem stories as they lend themselves easily to memorization and dramatization.

Example E: Choral poetry makes for a valuable class exercise. The possibilities are endless. Use your imagination, and ask the children to use theirs. The chorus can consist of the entire class, or small groups with solo parts.

EVALUATION: Poetry makes a wonderful avenue for drama. Right from kindergarten on, it helps children express themselves. It can be used to teach concepts, help memory skills, evoke feeling and understanding, deepen awareness, improve speech and oral communication skills, and stimulate the intuitive, creative attributes which all children have.

RESOURCES: The following are some of the better resource books that I have used:

Espy, Willard R., *A Children's Almanac of Words at Play*, Potter, N.Y., N.Y., 1982. A variety of everything having to do with words. 366 entries.

De La Mare, *Rhymes & Verses*, Holt, N.Y., N.Y., 47. Excellent variety of material for all ages.

Lear, Edward, *Nonsense Songs*, Warner & Co., London and N.Y. "Jumblies," "The Owl and The Pussycat," "Calico Pie," "Table and The Chair" are particularly good for acting out.

Cole, William, *Poems of Magic and Spells*, William Collins, Cleveland Ohio, 1977. This is excellent for a variety of magic. It is very appealing to children.

Hughes, Rosalind, *Let's Enjoy Poetry*, Houghton, 1958. This is the best resource for teachers. This book illustrates the proper way to read each poem, placing accents above the syllables which should be emphasized. It also gives appropriate teaching suggestions at the end of each poem.

Silverstein, *A Light in the Attic*, Harper & Row, 1974. This is a standard favorite; everyone uses it.

Opie, Peter, *The Oxford Nursery Rhyme Book*, excellent limericks and all.

POETRY — LONG NARRATIVE POEMS

GRADES: 4–8

TYPE OF ACTIVITY: Class presentation of a long narrative poem

GOALS:

1. To gain confidence from an oral presentation

2. To learn the appropriate use of voice both in volume and dramatic emphasis

3. To experience the cooperation, support, and teamwork which comes from a class presentation of this type

4. To enrich their vocabulary

5. To gain better historical perspective achieved by the emotional content of the poem and a discussion of the period and setting of the writing

READINESS: It is beneficial to review the reasons we need to learn how to best communicate with an audience. This will be an activity where children can help one another, compare in a positive way and improve their skill and confidence. The activity requires much self-discipline so it improves class tone.

PROCEDURE:

1. At least one hour should first be spent on introductory exercises and rules. A brief background may be given of the poem and further discussion may be done intermittently as the exercise proceeds.

2. A good beginning, after the warm-ups, is *Copy Me* (page 12). This would begin with the entire class copying the teacher, using pantomime at first. Once it is clear that the entire class is involved and concentrating, the voice can be used. This gives an opportunity to emphasize clear pronunciation and inflection with various speech exercises (see *page 23*).

3. Next, a student can be chosen to be leader for the *Copy Me* ac-

tivity, either on a random basis by observance of who is concentrating very intensely, or by asking for a volunteer.

4. Selection for the verses should be done at this time. First, each child will practice reading his verse so he can be sure of pronunciation and meaning. A time limit is set for completion of the memorization.

5. Emphasis for delivery should be made on the basis of consideration. The audience should not have to strain to hear or to understand. Try to encourage the use of gestures to help with getting the meaning across and to add dramatic interest. It also can add interest to the presentation to have certain lines repeated by the entire class. This is only for appropriate poems.

SPECIAL NEEDS: Include all members of the class regardless of capability.

EVALUATION: This is an excellent classroom activity which has many merits. One of the merits is that it is relatively easy and effective to use as a short performance piece. This gives all the children in the class a chance to participate almost equally, as well as to learn from each other. Class pride develops, and encouragement of the weaker ones ensues.

Narrative Poem Suggestions:

Paul Revere's Ride, Henry Wadsworth Longfellow
> One can incorporate a lot of early American history with this poem, and relate our early fight for freedom from British domination to present day conflicts which countries throughout the world are having for their freedom from foreign intervention.

John Gilpin, William Cowper
> This is a relatively easy poem, with measured meter and ample verses for a large class. There are some old English terms, such as eke, chaise and pair, agog, quoth, etc., which give a charming flavor to the poem, as well as give the opportunity for the children to enrich their vocabularies. There is ample opportunity for adding dramatic action to the stanzas as the selection is rich in onomatopoea and metaphor. The children seem to find it somewhat difficult to understand the story, so it's helpful to summarize it for them.

We, The People, Carl Sandburg
> This selection is challenging, but the results can be satisfying

and touching. It definitely could be used in connection with a further study of social studies, history, politics, literature or civics.

"The Spelling Bee at Angels Camp," Bret Harte;
  Cole, Wm., *Story Poems New and Old*
  This poem is very humorous and rich in onomatopoeic language, clever use of description words and passages, and dramatic dialogue. It could be considered an adjunct to English grammar and spelling suitable for fifth through eighth grade.

Poems of American History, Stevenson, Burton, ed.,
  Riverside Press, Cambridge, Mass, 1950.
  There is a great variety of suitable historical poems in this book. They cover every period of history from the discovery of America to recent times.

Hiawatha, Henry Wadsworth Longfellow
  This long narrative poem can be preceded by a discussion of the background of the American Indian, our Indian wars, and what ultimately happened to them. Longfellow wrote this poem as a tribute to and a protest against the tragedy of their loss. It is a beautiful poem, and one which is seldom studied in its entirety.

Child's Christmas in Wales, Dylan Thomas
  The language and imagery in this poem are inspiring. What a wonderful way to get a *feel* of another time, another culture! Children learn to paint pictures with their words, and to dramatize as they speak.

Casey at the Bat, Author unknown
  This group poem is fun to dramatize. Actors are chosen for individual parts, and it is always a favorite.

Beowulf, 8th century Northumbrian bard, unknown; drawn from Scandinavian history and folk source.
  This poem is rich in alliterative verse and gives rich pictures and exciting imagery as it recounts Beowulf's struggle with the water monster Grendel and his mother. Excellent for group work.

POOR KITTY

GRADES: K–4

TYPE OF ACTIVITY: Circle or line game, little movement, humorous

GOALS:
1. To provide an opportunity for children to be as silly as they like with a little *drama*

2. To help with control and concentration

3. To encourage shy children to participate

READINESS: Discuss *keeping control* and how difficult it is not to laugh when something is funny. Let them share their experiences where this has been a problem. Share a few of your own.

PROCEDURE:
1. Make a large circle and have someone volunteer to be in the middle.

2. The child will determine what kind of animal he wishes to be. He announces what he is, and then all the children in the circle are instructed to wipe the smiles off their faces. This is done with a stroke of the hand across the mouth, and they must keep that look, with no expression.

3. The actor in the middle looks around the circle and selects a likely candidate, moving appropriately in front of the child and proceeding to do his most amusing antics.

4. The child selected must look directly at the performer, pat him on the head three times, and say very slowly and distinctly, "Poor kitty, poor kitty, poor kitty." It could be frog, horse, dog, snake, or anything announced.

5. Should the child who is attempting to keep a straight face break his concentration and smile or laugh, he becomes *it* for the next game, and so we continue.

6. This game can also be done so that the winner is the child who does not smile and that child then has the option to be *it* or to choose someone.

VARIATION A: Be a clown; a teacher; a little child; or any character.

VARIATION B: Play the game with all the children standing facing the actor. They must sit when they smile.

SPECIAL NEEDS: Great for all, make sure that children with special needs are not left out.

EVALUATION: Great for informal role playing. Children love it!

PROPS

GRADES: K–8

TYPE OF ACTIVITY: This lesson involves the use of a variety of props to stimulate creativity.

GOALS:
1. To stimulate creativity.
2. To promote cooperation and group interaction.
3. To encourage the student to see multiple uses of the same object.

MATERIALS:
1. A variety of pieces of cloth.
2. Any object which is familiar, like a purse, chair, box or cup.
3. An unlikely object, such as a garbage cover, stone or branch.

READINESS: Explain the word *prop* as it is used in drama. It can be defined as an actual object which can be seen and touched. It also might be mentioned that frequently we don't use an actual prop but pretend the object is there with the use of pantomime.

PROCEDURE:
1. Have the students pretend to hold a glass of water, an ice cube, something sticky, a variety of objects.
2. Put a variety of props in front of the class ask for a volunteer to come up and demonstrate a way to use any one of the objects. Using the same object selected, ask for another volunteer to offer a different use for the same object.
3. Take a piece of cloth from the stack of varied pieces of material and ask for a variety of ideas as to ways this cloth could be used.
4. Put children in groups of 3 to 6 and give each group one prop with the instructions that they are to agree on a creative way to use it in a little mini-drama.

VARIATION A:	Give them 2 or 3 props.
VARIATION B:	Have them exchange with each other.
VARIATION C:	Let them select or make up their own.

EVALUATION: This is a wonderful lesson to be used as an "ice breaker," both for individual sharing or group work.

PROVERBS AND ADAGES

GRADES: 3–8

TYPE OF ACTIVITY: Dramas for small groups: writing, discussion and dramatization, art and music related

GOALS:
1. To become acquainted with some maxims or truths as a topic for discussion and drama.

2. To provide a subject to tie in with curriculum development, writing skills and memorization.

3. To enable children to work together creatively in small groups

4. To provide possible performance pieces for small or large audiences

READINESS: Proverbs and adages provide excellent material for a group discussion. They are part of our heritage, many being passed from generation to generation. Pick a few for group discussion and help them find the appropriate meaning to the words as applied to real life. Different meanings can be acceptable.

PROCEDURE:
1. Put one or two proverbs on the board and have a general discussion on their meaning and application.

2. Pass out the list of proverbs and give the class a period of quiet time to look them over. Suggest that they write down words which they don't understand, either on the board or a separate piece of paper.

3. Ask them to share one of their favorites and discuss it.

4. Give everyone a little time to write down their ideas for an anecdote that illustrates a proverb. This could be shared by having the class guess which proverb fits. For instance, a mother calls to her little girl, "You have a little tear in your dress. Come here and let me mend it," or "I'll have a bigger job tomorrow." Proverb: A stitch in time saves nine. These can be read, or acted out.

5. Put the children in small groups and let them work on a little mini-drama to illustrate a proverb of their choice or give each group a card with a proverb as an assignment.

VARIATION A: Have the children write their own scripts or make up their own proverbs.

VARIATION B: Word Mix-Up: Print the proverbs out on cards, cut the words apart, have the children try to put them together.

  a. Individually give a designated amount of time and see how many they can do.
  b. Have them work in groups of four to six.
  c. Have two teams.

VARIATION C: Make a memory game out of having the children study the list and then write down all the proverbs they remember.

EVALUATION: Children love doing these little mini-dramas. Values and morality are discussed and children are given an opportunity to express themselves appropriately. This lesson can be repeated at any grade level from 3rd grade on.

Proverbs and Adages

A bird in the hand is worth two in the bush.

A friend in need is a friend indeed.

A leopard can't change his spots.

A penny saved is a penny earned.

A rolling stone gathers no moss.

A stitch in time saves nine.

A watched pot never boils.

All things come to those who wait.

All work and no play makes Jack a dull boy.

An apple a day keeps the doctor away.

Beggars can't be choosers.

Better late than never.

Birds of a feather flock together.

Don't count your chickens before they're hatched.

Don't cry over spilt milk.

Don't make a mountain of a molehill.

Don't put all your eggs in one basket.

Great oaks from little acorns grow.

Haste makes waste.

If at first you don't succeed, try, try again.

It's a long road that has no turning.

Let sleeping dogs lie.

Little pitchers have big ears.

Make hay while the sun shines.

Measure twice and cut once.

Once burned, twice shy.

Out of the frying pan, into the fire.

Paddle your own canoe.

People who live in glass houses shouldn't throw stones.

Red sky in the morning, sailor take warning; red sky at night, sailors delight.

Seeing is believing.

Still waters run deep.

The early bird catches the worm.

Too many cooks spoil the broth.

Turnabout's fair play.

Two heads are better than one.

Two's company, three's a crowd.

Waste not, want not.

You can catch more flies with honey than with vinegar.

You can lead a horse to water, but you can't make him drink.

You can't eat your cake and have it, too.

You can't teach an old dog new tricks.

EVALUATION: This can become one of your favorite lessons. It has multiple uses: a springboard for discussion of values and real-life issues; the motivation for creative expression of all kinds; the potential for a performance theme.

QUAKER MEETING

GRADES: 3–8

TYPE OF ACTIVITY: Circle or line game, little movement

MATERIALS: Handy information on Quakers (see Readiness below); pictures if possible

GOALS:
1. To develop the ability to keep concentration and not laugh
2. To practice comedy-type techniques
3. To help with overcoming shyness
4. To improve posture

READINESS: It is first explained that *in the old days* children were expected to be ultra obedient! They sat up straight with their hands folded and their feet firmly placed on the floor. They were not allowed to show any expression on their faces, and were required to give full attention to the teacher at all times. A bit of religious background on the Quakers (*i.e., founded in 17th Century; believed in "inner light"; no intermediary; George Fox, who refused to give oaths or bear arms, was persecuted; settled first in Pennsylvania*) could be given as to how they got their name, where they came from, why they came to this country, and even how they influenced education.

PROCEDURE:
1. Children are instructed to sit up straight and give their full attention to the performer, who will try his best to distract or amuse them and get them to smile.
2. This little verse is said in unison before the actor begins:

> Quaker Meeting has begun.
> No more laughter, no more fun!
> If you show your teeth or tongue,
> You shall pay a forfeit!

3. The actor then says it alone and tries to get someone to *lose his or her cool.*

4. The forfeit can be simply that the child who breaks first and smiles or loses attention will be the next actor, or it could be some agreed-upon penalty. The winner is the one or ones who do not smile, as the others are eliminated when they smile.

VARIATION: **Old Fashioned Spelling Test:** Using the same theme of "Quaker" type behavior, have the children stand up straight, hands behind their back and they must repeat the word, spell it, repeat it again, or they miss. this must be done without a smile. Children of all ages love it!

SPECIAL NEEDS: This game affords a good opportunity to discuss accepting *differences.*

EVALUATION: Popular; fun and with excellent benefits. Children of all ages love this game. It promotes good feelings and self-control.

READING ALOUD — DRAMATIC

GRADES: 3–8

TYPE OF ACTIVITY: Dramatic reading, individual, involving whole class

GOALS:
1. To give children a chance to improve their oral reading skills

2. To learn to give critical and fair evaluations, thereby benefiting from helpful criticism

3. To have fun while learning an important skill

READINESS: Have a good discussion about oral skills in general; how the speaker needs to use a considerate voice, make eye contact and use appropriate body language. *Appropriate*, meaning that whether one sits or stands — moves around or stays still, uses gestures or not, the body language should *help* with the communication and not distract. As much as possible, elicit responses from the children — so *they* think about it.

PROCEDURE:
1. Request that they prepare a short *dramatic* reading one or two minutes long at most.

2. First there should be a discussion about what is meant by a *dramatic* reading. Look for these comments:

   • One with expression and feeling
   • One with descriptive words
   • Maybe dialogue and parts to act out
   • Stress that they are to attempt to hold the attention of the audience, using whatever means they feel appropriate.

3. Make this an assignment either leaving class time for preparation or as homework.

4. Every child in class can have a grading card, and as each student goes up to present his reading, each member of the audience is to score him from one to ten, ten being the top score (optional.)

5. A variation to using the grading card is to hold up the hands: five fingers represents the lowest, and ten the highest.

6. Comments are also encouraged, to be noted both on the paper and also offered aloud; again, the comments are to be only about what we liked and what made the reading effective. Later there can be helpful general statements which indicate those things which need improvement.

EVALUATION: This assignment is particularly good to repeat as often as possible, because the students learn from each other and thus are motivated to improve this very important skill. Teachers, at all grade levels from 3rd on up, found the activity to be one of their favorites.

ROLE PLAYING

GRADES: 1–8

TYPE OF ACTIVITY: Role playing involving whole class — problem solving

GOALS:

1. To teach children to look at themselves

2. To teach children to look at the actions and behavior of others

3. To help children attempt to put themselves in someone else's place and thus experience their own feelings and thoughts

4. To have open discussions which are a logical outcome of role plays. This helps establish rules of behavior and a code of ethics

5. To discuss and better understand social life

6. To bring history and social studies to life for the children when they dramatize and role play the people and events used in their study

READINESS: Role playing can be used in the classroom to make it a real-life laboratory for social and academic learning. The unique advantage of role playing is that it affords students an opportunity to practice new behaviors by *doing* and not just *thinking*. The ideas for doing come from the students' own imaginations, the suggestions of their peers, or the prompting of the teacher. The important thing is that the student is *being someone else* and can safely experiment with all sorts of different ways to meet pervasive problems and conflicts. This method helps develop critical thinking and problem-solving skills. Academic material is thereby enriched, and this provocative classroom technique can be a stepping stone to many other related activities.

We note how people react to us and interpret how they feel, but all too often we misinterpret their behavior and draw damaging conclusions. This is one of the most common causes of interpersonal conflict. It helps if a person can put himself in someone else's place and thus appreciate the other's feelings and thoughts. He may better understand how his behavior affects others and why they behave toward him as they do. With this awareness, the child may be able to effect changes in behavior so that social interaction and feelings about himself are improved. Role-playing is an ideal way to demonstrate that hostility and suspicion stimulate hostile and defensive reactions in others, whereas generosity and tolerance stimulate constructive social behavior.

PROCEDURE:

1. It is helpful to start with clearly stated rules, warm-ups and introduction exercises. This sets the tone and gives the children some non-threatening experience with drama.

2. Select the problem or situation pertinent to the issue or academic material. This can be done either by the teacher or the class depending on the issue and goals.

3. Select and brief the actors and explain briefly, but in as much detail as possible, the specific role each child is to play.

4. Delineate the very important role of the audience, which is to be considerate, attentive, and responsive. These students can be instructed to observe the general interaction or charged to watch for specific actors or events. Sometimes it is more beneficial, however, to give no directions to the audience other than the rules for proper audience behavior, and to begin with a more spontaneous approach. This decision depends on the general purpose which the classroom teacher has in mind.

5. The next stage will consist of the actual drama and subsequent discussion of the action. These role plays should be long enough for the students to become thoroughly immersed in the situation, as this will give them a better opportunity to discover alternative ways of acting.

6. The discussion can be handled several different ways; audience reaction and suggestion, actor/participant reaction and suggestion, or breaking the class up into small groups for interaction and analysis.

7. A final important focus of this learning experience would be the application of the lesson to real life and the children's own personal experience.

8. The teacher and pupils discuss and evaluate the success or failure of this experience. This should be based primarily on two things: The accuracy of the roles which the participants attempted to portray and the degree of concentration or distraction. With regard to the accuracy of the roles, there should be a discussion about the effect these roles had on the actors, as well as the audience. It is very important that a constant attempt be made on the part of the entire class to take this exercise seriously. Laughter is fine, as long as it is appropriate, and this is sometimes a delicate matter. Some of the role-playing may be extremely humorous, and this gives the actor-participants an opportunity to really concentrate and attempt to stay with their role. It also gives the class the opportunity to practice the key rule, *Be Considerate*, because otherwise the safe atmosphere will be lost, as well as the effectiveness of the exercise.

EVALUATION & BENEFITS: This is an excellent lesson for a number of reasons: role-playing provides a broad format for teaching drama skills; it gives children an opportunity to interact, express feelings, evaluate and problem-solve and attempt to understand others. Social studies, as well as other subjects such as science and math can be enlivened and enriched with the roleplay of situations and real people. It decreases the gap between thinking and doing.

Easy and Fun Role Plays
1. Psychiatrist and patient (with a problem)
2. Teacher and student (troublesome)
3. Teacher and principal (dissatisfied)
4. Santa Claus and child
5. Parent and child (with a bad report card or a problem)
6. *Pusher* (drugs) and child
7. Teacher and parent
8. Two parents discussing problem
9. Two children getting to know one another — different age; different race; different country, etc.
10. Sibling rivalry
11. Shoplifter and arresting officer
12. Any person from history facing a particular situation discussing the ramifications of their decision

It is especially fun and beneficial to have them reverse roles. A line can be made and they simply take turns.

(More than 2)

1. A group of young mothers talking about their children
2. A team getting psyched up to win a game; after winning; after losing
3. Teenagers discussing their first dates
4. Girls deciding what to wear; makeup; hairstyle
5. Teachers discussing their classes
6. Students discussing their classes
7. Students waiting to go to principal's office
8. An *in-group* not wanting to include an outsider, some designated *for* and some *against*
9. A group picking on new child in school; one or two defending
10. Parents discussing problems they are having with children
11. Peer pressure to wear a particular type of clothing, go to an inappropriate place, cheat on an exam, shoplift, vandalize, etc.
12. Any aspect of social studies or history: immigrants and their problems, the westward movement, the Indians' feelings, and so forth

The possibilities are endless. These are great fun to do. Students must be cautioned not to talk all at once but to *be considerate* to their audience.

SCIENCE & DRAMA — WHOLE CLASS & SMALL GROUP

GRADES: 1–8

TYPE OF ACTIVITY: Drama is used to stimulate the intuitive and creative attributes which all children have in relation to science

GOALS:
1. To broaden and deepen scientific understandings
2. To give children an opportunity to use their creative abilities
3. To provide problem-solving opportunities
4. To provide a performance piece having science as a theme

READINESS: Science can be made exciting and meaningful through the use of drama. Adults, working with children, mainly need to provide some of the basic tools, but most of all, it is faith and enthusiastic encouragement and involvement to which young people respond so well. Consequently they become willing to use their innate intuitive abilities.

PROCEDURE:
1. Basic rules should be reviewed and some warm up exercises done, as this will remind the children of their responsibilities, both as audience and as participants (see *Five Things*, page 36; *Audience/Actor*, page 3; *Warm-ups* page 19).

2. Children can be put in groups of four to six and asked to come up with a creative and dramatic way to present a scientific subject. They are given a specific amount of class time, for the rough idea to be shown to the rest of the class.

3. For this approach, the matter of further ideas can be left open for homework, or extra class time, for the children to get together and write songs, poems, skits, art work, or anything pertaining to the subject.

4. Ideas seed more ideas, so class time needs to be scheduled for the presentations as they get ready. Helpful criticism is given,

both regarding what is good and what might need some improvement.

Example A: Geology — A fifth grade class used their study of rocks to springboard them into a major show featuring a young pianist accompanying the class in *Rock Around the Clock*, dancers dubbing themselves *The Volcanics*, original costumes to represent the various rocks, together with verse. Skits, poems, originality and talent abounded. Many insecure students gained confidence.

Example B: Astronomy — A fifth grade class used their study of astronomy as a basis for a show. The *Big Bang Theory* was dramatized to the music of 2001, as the children spun off to form planets and then created their own rock number with original dialogue stating facts about their planet. See: *Our Solar System* (page 94) for primary.

Example C: Anatomy — Children were put in small groups and asked to come up with a skit representing some part of the human body: heart, nose, respiratory system, digestive system, brain, circulatory system. Their creativity was astonishing and informative. An excellent show was put together culminating with *Dem Bones* and dancing with a real skeleton! (The teacher participated in the dance.)

Example D: Biology — The following shows are musicals with ample dialogue, tapes and scores. None are too difficult and all have been performed very successfully:

- *Goin Buggy*, Jill Galina (delightful musical about insects — primary)
- *Rx for Earth*, Joyce Merman (solutions for children)
- *Gonna Have An Earth Day*, Mary Lynn Lightfoot (environmental — any age)
- *Dinosaur Valley*, Betty Barlow and Joyce Merman (ecology and fun)

- *Assignment Earth (what kids can do to save the planet)*, Roger Emerson

All shows can be ordered by contacting *Pepper Catalog* 1-800-345-6296.

EVALUATION: Regardless of the choice made and whether the performance is major or minimal, the results have been universally beneficial. There is *sometimes* a period where children resist the discipline and work, but *always* all are happy with the results. The class *comes together* and individual children blossom. Parents and the community are particularly enthusiastic about the application of the curriculum to drama and creativity, and frequently volunteer assistance and financial support to general building funds.

SCIENCE — IMPROVISATIONAL DRAMA

GRADES: 3–8

TYPE OF ACTIVITY: Dramatizing and improvising scientific concepts: small group and individual and whole class

GOALS: 1. To help children internalize scientific concepts by the use of their bodies and visual tools

2. To encourage students to do problem solving and think creatively

3. To add another dimension to the learning process

READINESS: Each subject can be preceded by a brief discussion which will help review and stimulate academic knowledge, encourage open discussions and creative solutions.

PROCEDURE: 1. A few examples follow and may be used in any number of improvisational ways:

Example A: Electricity — Have the children demonstrate with their bodies: AC current; DC current; a complete circuit, static electricity; lightning; magnetism; positive/negative poles; a conductor, etc.

Example B: Make a list of words and have the children pantomime whatever the words make them think of. First, have the entire class participate, with the reminder that they are not to look at one another; then, split the class and have comments and evaluations. This will provide stimulus for further ideas.

Sample words: evaporation, condensation, magnetic, photosynthesis, tornado, circulation, fusion, etc.

Example C: Put appropriate concept ideas on the board, have the children work by themselves, in pairs or in small groups to demonstrate. Use puzzling things, and reassure them that their hypotheses need not be 100% accurate, but somewhat reasonable. Some examples are:

- Demonstrate gravity
- What causes the wind to blow?
- What causes a storm?
- What causes an earthquake?
- How does the brain work?
- What is magnetism?
- How do things grow?
- What causes the tides?
- How are the different rocks formed?
- What's the difference between a planet and a star?

EVALUATION: There is no end of ideas and children should be encouraged to come up with their own. The discussion after each presentation stimulates the desire for more knowledge on the subject. These are valuable activities, and are fun to do.

SCIENCE AND PERSONALITIES

GRADES: 3–8

TYPE OF ACTIVITY: Monologues and dialogues based on important people in the field, with displays and demonstrations

GOALS: 1. To motivate children to learn more about a subject

2. To personalize someone famous so the student can identify

3. To individualize capabilities and talents

READINESS: Sometimes intellectual children are labeled *eggheads* or *nerds* or whatever is current. This activity helps dispel that notion and give credit and respect to some of our truly great heroes; people who have saved lives, made *our* lives better and had values other than material gain.

PROCEDURE: 1. Ask each child to pick a scientist or inventor, research that person, and write as though they were the person.

2. Have a suggested list, but allow latitude and encourage special interests.

3. If possible, try to conference with each child in order to match them with a famous person who might somehow represent a personal special interest.

4. As much as possible, encourage the student to try to take on the personality of their subject, and to look for those things in their individual lives that they felt contributed to that personality.

5. If it is possible to *show* or *tell* or *do* some of their early experiments or discoveries, this will add interest to their presentations.

6. Costumes, charts, art work, displays are optional.

7. A variation could be an interview which would involve question and answer.

EVALUATION: Famous scientists provide a wealth of real life heroes. When the children identify with and personalize their subjects, they help bring the persons to life, both for themselves and for the class. A number of traveling scientists were selected to go around to other classes, which stimulated others to want to do a similar lesson. This is always a particularly successful project.

SITUATIONS

GRADES: 1–8

TYPE OF ACTIVITY: Whole group, active, pantomime and voice

GOALS:
1. To use imagination
2. To stimulate creativity
3. To improve concentration
4. To tie in emotions, actions, voice, characterization, and all things into a spontaneous improvisation

READINESS: Discuss how our emotions determine our actions and vice versa. Bring up some situations as examples, and ask for ideas from the children.

PROCEDURE:
1. Start with one of the other pantomime exercises, or even the Freeze Game, to loosen them up.
2. Call out situations, reminding them not to look at one another.
3. Freeze, and bring to life when appropriate

VARIATION A:	Divide into Audience/Actor and have comments.
VARIATION B:	Ask for volunteers to be the director and have them call out ideas of their own.
VARIATION C:	Make it a homework assignment for them to make out a list of situations to act out.
VARIATION D:	Look in magazines or wherever action pictures can readily be found. Show them to the children as a stimulus for action. Ask them to look for pictures also.

SPECIAL NEEDS: All children should be included. This activity is very therapeutic.

EVALUATION: Invaluable for fun and training. Imagination, creativity and concentration improve each time we do this. Children become increasingly involved with these activities and bring in ideas of their own.

Examples of Situations:

1. Candy or gum stuck to bottom of pants
2. Drink your soup; Fly in soup
3. Fingers stuck in bowling ball
4. Snowball melting in hand
5. Cactus thorns in back
6. Carry twenty heavy books or anything heavy; drop it
7. Someone dumps grease on you
8. Chew twenty pieces of gum
9. Someone put ice or snow down your back
10. Wearing braces; put foil in mouth (shock)
11. Spilled blackberries on best white outfit
12. Step on bubble gum; get it on hands, all over
13. Ants in shoes, shirt, etc.
14. You have a baby in arms: won't sleep; dropped
15. Blow bubble gum bubble; it breaks; all over your face and hair
16. Have pie fight
17. Drink a hot cup of hot chocolate
18. Hold wet frog
19. Squashed worm in hand
20. Skunk behind you
21. Step in mud puddle
22. Sit down on, or touch, wet paint
23. Put on shorts or pants; too tight
24. Step on a banana peel
25. Watching favorite TV program: funny; sad; scary; TV breaks
26. Try on dress; It rips
27. Trying to carry bag of feathers; they fly out
28. Hiccups; can't get rid of them
29. You have poison oak; it itches; can't scratch
30. Drunk and trying to act sober; walk straight

31. Have pillow fight; feathers in nose

32. You knocked over your mother's best vase, glued it together, and now it's leaking all over the dinner table.

33. You just stepped in some mushy mud with your best shoes on; with your bare feet

34. Your brother or sister just tracked mud on your mother's best rug, and you are getting the blame.

35. You are cooking and everything starts to burn as your mother comes home.

36. You're the only one home and the washer is overflowing, the teakettle is boiling and the baby is crying.

37. You just popped a water balloon all over yourself; and a partner

38. A giant spider is crawling up your leg and you are in a situation where you can't reach down to get it off (eg., at a party, in a play, etc.)

39. A hippopotamus just stepped on your toe.

40. You disobey a *Do NOT Feed the Animals* sign at the zoo and realize that the zookeeper is watching you.

41. You are in a play or choir and accidentally sing off cue.

42. Someone told you to look closely at a book and then snapped it closed on you.

43. You find your favorite record got warped (or tape tangled.)

44. You found a bug in your food.(You specify the bug and the food.)

45. You are an animal of your choice.

46. You must walk on hot sand or on ice in bare feet.

47. You are in a play and the curtain is about to rise when you realize your forgot something important: your lines, a prop, your costume, or other.

48. You have a very bad sunburn and someone slaps you on the back

49. You are a musical instrument. Now play the instrument.

50. You are a color. Respond to the color (blue, black, green, red, etc.).

51. You find yourself in a land of giants who try to step on you.

52. You just finished a huge dinner and feel stuffed.

53. You die in an unusual way (make it unusual *and* funny):

- You accidentally cut your throat while playing the violin.
- You get locked in a stall shower and drown.
- You die from overeating, or from a passion for chocolates.
- You are swallowed by a man-eating flower.
- You tie a tie or scarf too tight by accident.
- You get trapped in a swimsuit that is too tight.
- You sink in quicksand.

54. You are waiting at the doctor's office for a shot you don't want.

55. You are dying of thirst.

56. All the toys in your room suddenly come to life. You *are* the toy come to life.

57. You are extremely sleepy but must force yourself to get up for an important event.

58. You get lost in a jungle, on a beach, in a crowded store, etc.

59. You bite into an apple and find half a worm.

60. You are asleep and having a bad nightmare

61. You just burned yourself on a hot stove.

62. You are seasick.

63. You are trying to write a composition but can think of nothing. You keep daydreaming.

64. You are at a new school and all the kids seem mean.

65. You laugh uncontrollably in a serious situation and must try to stop yourself, but you can't.

66. You get a huge gob of peanut butter stuck to your mouth.

67. You just got a spanking for something you didn't do.

68. All your friends are angry at you.

69. You are trying to get a cute person to like you.

70. You lose the grocery money your mother gave you.

71. You just got a tooth filled with a double dose of novocaine and your mouth feels like a balloon.

72. You're stuck in a glass cage; under water; falling endlessly through the sky

73. Someone just told you horrible news. Someone just told you good news.

74. Your body is a huge rubber band; it is made of glass; it is made of bricks; it is made of water; it is made of thick

syrup; it is made of sand; it is made of yarn; it is made of wire.

75. You wake up to find: you are a cockroach; you are seven feet tall; you are one foot tall.

76. You just broke your dad's stereo; your friend's violin

77. You just found out your best friend is going out with your boyfriend (or girlfriend).

78. You just stole a handful of cookies and your mother was watching.

79. You just fell down and skinned your knee a long way from home.

80. You just stepped on a slug in bare feet.

81. You get a live bug in your ear.

82. You walk into a dark room with cobwebs, and can't find your way out.

83. You are in an elevator that gets stuck.

84. You lost important homework on the way to school.

85. You have to show a bad report to your parents and try to explain.

86. You see someone being picked on and go to defend.

87. You are being picked on because you're new and different.

88. You are a peddler, selling your wares.

89. You are kind and thoughtful and trying to soothe someone who is angry.

90. You are an old person, young ones run by and splash mud on you and you scold them.

91. You are a balloon salesman. You sell some to children and several get away.

92. You open and read a letter. It contains bad news; good news.

93. You are in a school play and got a bad part; the lead part

94. Stuck door; get it open; treasure room; enjoy; door jams; trapped; no way out; find window; pound; scream; break window; cut hand; help comes

95. Go in mother's room; try on necklace; diamond earrings; be a fancy lady; lose one earring; mother comes home; frantic search; find it; play innocent

96. You are walking: through very deep snow; on hot sand;

on marbles; through fallen leaves; in sticky mud; in waves on the beach; on dangerous ground; in a dark cave; on the moon; climbing a mountain

97. You are eating: a drippy ice cream cone; some potato chips; a lemon; a lollipop; something sticky; cotton candy; something you love; something you hate; a hot drink; a very cold drink

98. You have: walked a very long distance and it's 100 degrees in the shade; a blister on your heel; a rock in your shoe.

99. You are trying to: lift some barbells, a heavy object; drag this object; carry something without spilling it: a pail of water, a tray, two glasses

100. You come into a room and accidentally disturb everyone. You are late for school.

SKITS

GRADES: 2–8

TYPE OF ACTIVITY: Involves acting and small group work

GOALS:
1. To provide an opportunity for cooperative effort and for leadership qualities to emerge
2. To give an opportunity for creative activity
3. To have children begin to learn what is effective with an audience
4. To assist with problem-solving ability
5. To get practice with improvisation
6. To help develop curriculum subjects

READINESS: Remind children of the one rule: *Be Considerate!* and do *not* hurt anyone's feelings by acting as though you don't want to be in his group.

PROCEDURE:
1. Group the children. Try to provide new associations. Groups of three work well. If groups are four, five or six, sometimes a leader is chosen. If the children pick their own groups, tell them that they must leave no one out.
2. Give them a subject (see Variations), a time length for the skit, and allow a short time for planning (five to ten minutes.)
3. As groups get ready, give them a sequential number, as this encourages them to finish more quickly.
4. Once preparations time is up, call everyone to come and be the audience.
5. Reassure any groups who are not yet ready that you will give them an *on the spot* idea and that it's no one's fault but simply happens that way at times.

VARIATION A: **Subject Skit** — Subject skits are ideal for almost any purpose. There is no end to the possibilities for a subject, from drug problems to home and school problems. Science subjects, such as astronomy, geology and anatomy provide the children with an opportunity for unbounded creativity. Social studies in any area from mythology to westward movement give children opportunity for spontaneous or planned skits, based on classroom needs. Math, grammar, vocabulary, and virtually any subject area can be creatively dramatized. (See subject areas in Table of Contents.)

VARIATION B: **Prop Skit** — These skits allow the use of a prop and show how creatively a prop can be used. Any single prop can be used, such as a shawl, a garbage cover, or a ruler, and the groups are told to incorporate the prop in their skits. Another variation is to put a number of objects in front of the room and let each child or group select one to use as desired. This activity is fun, and it gives children a focus, as well as creative ways to use props.

VARIATION C: **Phrase** — Give them a phrase as a theme for the skit. This may either be a theme or the instructions are to end their skit with the phrase as a *Freeze*.

Examples:
- *Wow! That's great!*
- *I don't believe it!*
- *Friends are fickle.*
- *Not again!*
- *Do I have to?*
- *Seeing is believing.*

The possibilities are endless!

VARIATION D: **Trapped or Problem Skit** — Choose the children at random for this activity; mix boys and girls, and provide a suitable mixture of talents and friendships. This is a quickie, and I only allow a few minutes for them to think of a problem or a situation in which they are trapped. This can be with or without a solution. The first time through they need to do it in pantomime. The second time, if time allows, they may use voice and introductions. This exercise is extremely helpful for a number of reasons, one of the most important being the cooperation it engenders and the audience involvement required in order to *guess* the problem when it is done in pantomime.

VARIATION E: **Group Pantomime Cards** — It's handy to keep a box of cards with different ideas printed on the cards which you can hand to the group, or just show them, and then ask that they spontaneously perform what is suggested on the card. The audience then guesses what is happening. The following are some examples which work particularly well for this purpose:

You are all:

- in a terrible storm (tornado, hurricane, electric, snow…).
- at a football game; the score is close.
- inspecting a haunted house and are very frightened.
- arguing about where to go and what to do.
- tossing one ball back and forth.
- at the beach.
- watching an air show…, a kite flying contest.
- in a boat which is leaking.
- waiting to see the principal due to some offense or broken rule.
- at a party.

  Once these have been done in pantomime, they can be repeated out loud.

EVALUATION: This activity, done in any number of varieties, is wonderful, not only for the cooperative effort which leads to better class tone, but also much valuable learning takes place. Children love the interaction.

SOCIAL STUDIES — COUNTRIES

GRADES: 4–8

TYPE OF ACTIVITY: Study of a country's culture and history, using drama; small group and individual

GOALS:
1. To increase children's confidence and ability to communicate effectively to an audience

2. To help children gain a deeper understanding of a foreign country and culture

3. To encourage children to use their own ingenuity and problem-solving techniques

4. To give children an opportunity to use their particular talents for their presentation: art, music, dance, drama, etc.

5. To enable children to effectively evaluate each other's performance

READINESS: Review some of the material which has already been covered about countries studied. This is an appropriate time to have a discussion about ethnic backgrounds leading into ideas coming from the children themselves as to how they can celebrate their diversity (see variation at end of lesson)

PROCEDURE:
1. This is a full class activity. Some time should be spent on introductory exercises, rules and group work.

2. Suggested topics could be put on the board or given as a handout. Encourage ideas from the students and add appropriate ones to the list.

3. Some of the possibilities for methods of presentation are: monologue; dramatic scene; use of pictures, charts and music; and dialogue giving information. Discuss and ask for further suggestions.

4. The next step could be to have each student write down his individual ideas which can be further developed by requiring five to ten *facts* to be written down about each idea.

5. An alternate approach is to group the children and have them come up with their own ideas, perhaps appointing one person as the secretary to write everything down.

6. Viewing of the preliminary skits should begin as soon as possible. They are told that their presentation need not be perfected, but if they can give a rough idea, they will get helpful feedback from classmates and teachers. Emphasis should be on *being considerate* to the audience, so that their presentation is both informative, clear and entertaining.

7. Actual presentation can be as elaborate or simple as desired. Decision can be made on the degree of involvement within the class.

VARIATION A:	A treasure chest can be kept in the classroom and children encouraged to bring in ethnic treasures from home. Great care should be taken with these objects and they can be used in any number of creative ways or as take off for study of maps, countries, food, folk tales, etc. with an emphasis on both similarities and differences.
VARIATION B:	An ethnic celebration can be planned by the class with tables set out to represent different countries and backgrounds. Children do their own planning, together with assistance from parents, and creatively present their displays. Groups of children work well together on projects of this kind. Presentation can be either formal or informal.

EVALUATION: These ideas are appropriate for any grade level from fourth through eighth grades. It is a very effective way to augment the teaching of social studies and the study of a particular country or period of time. It could even be done by a primary grade, but on a much simpler lever. The benefits are inestimable and the resulting satisfaction felt by all, far outweighs the effort put out for the project.

SOCIAL STUDIES — NATIVE AMERICAN CULTURE

GRADES: 2–8

TYPE OF ACTIVITY: Dramatic activities to augment the study of native Americans

GOALS:
1. To internalize a better appreciation of another culture
2. To give children an opportunity to use all their creative skills along with their curriculum study

READINESS: There should be some discussion of the term *native American* and why our American Indian prefers that title. Children should be aware that this country belonged to the Indians so they really are the only *natives*. Background material can be geared to appropriate age level and the discretion of the teacher. Encourage the children to find out what they can about Indian history and have them share with the class.

PROCEDURE: There are many ways to enrich curriculum study. Some ideas are as follows:

1. Indian legends. Read some to the class and encourage them to read on their own. Have them write their own legends. Act the legends out in groups or have the author read orally and select roles to be improvised.

2. Introduce Haiku poetry.[1] Have children compose and read aloud.

3. Have the class study the poem *Hiawatha* by Longfellow. This can be done as a choral poem with each child memorizing a section and some lines repeated in unison. (see *Choral Poetry* in Table of Contents)

4. Use *Twelve Moons*, Ruth Roberts, Michael Brent, Publishers, Inc.[2]

EVALUATION: There are many more ways to enrich the study of native Americans but these suggestions have been tried and true. Performances have been both elaborate and simple. Both ways have merit. We have done a number of mini-shows with Kindergarten classes using the native American theme. Costumes are easily put together, usually in the classroom as an art project. Sometimes parents or resource people help, even just to make drums, rattles, or teach Indian games.

---

[1] Haiku: Unrhymed Japanese poem recording the essence of a keenly perceived moment linking nature and human nature. Three line poem of five, seven, and five syllables

[2] Twelve Moons dramatizes the evolution of the Indian from the time of the dinosaurs through their way of life and change, the coming of the white man, the loss of their culture, and hope for the future. The music, story telling, and drama are excellent.

SOCIAL STUDIES — NATIVE AMERICAN CULTURE

GRADES: K–1

TYPE OF ACTIVITY: Group activity and presentation to augment native American study, involving pantomime, drama and music

GOALS:
1. To internalize a better appreciation of another culture
2. To incorporate art, music, and drama into a simple performance piece
3. To give small children a chance to attempt a cooperative effort, as well as give individual responses

READINESS: The study of native Americans and their unique culture can begin early. Discourage the *war whoop* and *cowboy and Indian* approach which may be the children's first response. Children can easily *imagine* themselves in tune with nature, understanding the animal and plant kingdom, and fitting their needs into some degree of harmony. They love the sign language, picture talk, legends, costumes and all aspects of this rich culture.

PROCEDURE:
1. Give the children some background, in a simple way, of the Indian culture, which was so richly in harmony with nature.
2. Have the children do all kinds of pantomime warm ups, such as being animals, trees, flowers, birds, weather, etc.
3. Mini-show is as follows:
   - Children walk in with dignity (straight posture), arms crossed in front and stand on stage.
   - Leader (teacher or older child) does some *Copy Me*, relating to Indian sign language: welcome, peace, sun, storm, horse, long journey, etc.
   - Song or Indian chant.
   - Children follow the leader out onto the floor or a more

spacious area and disperse themselves with a *Freeze*, like an Indian hunting, gathering, fishing.

- Pantomime scenes can be done where the children are asked to do any appropriate activity such as: net a fish, paint a tepee, grind some corn, plant the corn, see an eagle's nest, pick berries, shoot a bow and arrow, walk silently like an Indian, etc.

5. The presentation should be short (ten to fifteen minutes), flexible, and relaxed. With small children, anything can happen, so be prepared to assist in any way necessary. Above all, try to make it a pleasant, non-threatening experience for them.

EVALUATION: This presentation is a favorite with this age group. Costuming is as simple or complex as desired. Complexity is designed to fit the group but has endless possibilities. I have used this format many times in my teaching.

SPEAKER AND ACTOR

GRADES: 2–8

TYPE OF ACTIVITY: Working in pairs; it involves acting and speaking; communication skill development

GOALS:
1. To promote dramatic speaking and story telling techniques
2. To teach children to pause, and allow listeners to form pictures in their minds
3. To encourage clarity and proper voice control
4. To improve oral reading techniques
5. To allow children an opportunity to dramatize simple scenes
6. To promote good feelings and have fun

READINESS: Discuss those things which are necessary in order to be a good *story teller*. Ask, "What do we use when we speak to an audience?" (eye contact, voice control, hands and body gestures, feelings, expressions, pauses.) Draw the responses from the children if possible. Remind them that this skill will take practice.

PROCEDURE:
1. Ask for two volunteers. Designate one the speaker and one the actor.

2. Instruct the speaker to come up with a simple scene or just a sentence or two. Almost anything will do. For example:
   - "A little girl was walking down the road when she stopped and picked up something. She was surprised and happy. It was a $5.00 bill."
   - Another way to start is, "Once upon a time…"
   - If the story teller wants his actor to speak, he simply says, "…and then she said…" and waits. This technique is almost 100 percent successful.

3. They will reverse their roles, so each gets an opportunity to experience both parts. Select new volunteers, or each pair can choose a replacement.

VARIATION A: Use books or poems, and ask that they look for a dramatic passage to act out. Stress that it should be short.

VARIATION B: Put them in pairs to plan their short scenes. They could even write it out as a mini-script.

SPECIAL NEEDS: *All* children should attempt this exercise, but if it is too difficult for some, ask that they be the audience.

EVALUATION: This definitely is a marvelous exercise to help children with both speech and oral reading. It seems to help them develop the proper pauses, inflection of voice, and audience contact. It's so much fun that children of all ages want to repeat it again and again.

SPONTANEOUS SPEAKING

GRADES: 2–8

TYPE OF ACTIVITY: Verbal, individual: promoting speaking ability

GOALS:
1. To promote a more natural speaking ability
2. To develop acting talent
3. To give confidence.

READINESS: Discuss how emotion contributes to speech. Demonstrate the different feelings one can put to a word such as "Wow", "I don't believe it". Let the class experiment.

PROCEDURE:
1. Ask for volunteers. Give them a word, such as, *shoe, desk any* word and then tell them to say *anything* even repeating the word over and over if necessary.

2. Side-coach by saying, "Speak happy, sad, proud, angry," etc.

3. Have them try the same thing *without* a special word; just use the emotion.

4. Assign characters. Speak like a *teacher, parent, principal, child,* etc.

5. Add a situation to the character:
   - An angry teacher with a bad class.
   - A parent scolding a child.
   - A principal giving rules.
   - A child's first day in school, etc.

6. Have them do familiar story-book characters —
   - Big bad wolf
   - Cinderella, Goldilocks, Papa Bear

EVALUATION: The more this is done, the more children want to try it. Each time they go up they get better and better. This can be used for a performance piece.

STATUE

GRADES: 1–5

TYPE OF ACTIVITY: Done in pairs for entire group; stationary; little movement

GOALS:
1. To promote good feelings — a *hands on* activity
2. To increase skill in *The Freeze*
3. To promote imagination and creativity

READINESS: Discuss being considerate of *feelings*, as this exercise will particularly require it.

PROCEDURE:
1. Pair the class off; the children decide who is No. 1 and who is No. 2.

2. Instruct all the No. 1s to make a *ball* out of themselves. They are then the *clay* and No. 2s are all *sculptors*.

3. Give them a theme — usually a *feeling* works well, such as hunger, joy, love, fear, or something like that.

4. The sculptors are given the theme and about three to five minutes to create their statues. The *lump of clay* is instructed *not* to move, except when being formed by their artist. Naturally, they cannot talk or they'll be disqualified.

5. At the end of the designated time, the sculptors are all instructed to come over and stand aside. We all view the statues at this point, and if we have no other judges, ask the sculptors to be the judges.

6. Stand next to each statue, asking for applause, and requesting that although they are to applaud for each one, their favorite should get the most applause.

7. Next, reverse and the sculptors become the *clay*. It also works very well and adds interest to have three or four children be

lumps of clay and the sculptors can then create even more complex and interesting statues.

SPECIAL NEEDS: Include all, unless there is obvious strong resistance, in which case a child can be included by allowing him to help judge.

EVALUATION: Marvelous! Really promotes good feelings. This exercise is excellent for a performance piece. Parents and friends love it.

STUDENT/TEACHER — SCRIPTS FROM LITERATURE

GRADES: 3–8

TYPE OF ACTIVITY: Involves reading a work of literature and helping children develop a script to dramatize

TIME 10–12 hours

MATERIALS: Literature selection — text for all students

GOALS:
1. To deepen appreciation and enthusiasm for a work of literature
2. To stimulate script writing
3. To give children an opportunity to be good story tellers and actors
4. To learn how to work as a team, be good sports, and ultimately have a satisfying show piece

READINESS: Select a book for a reading. Some books lend themselves better than others to this technique as the more varied and colorful the characters, the better. Examples of excellent works: *James and the Giant Peach; Tom Sawyer; The Hobbit; Treasure Island.*

PROCEDURE:
1. Each week, as a portion of the book is assigned, have someone volunteer to *tell the story*, covering the pages which the class has read. The story teller can choose the main characters, and even have children play parts like bushes, walls, trees, or birds. The story teller controls the action. The actors pantomime, and when the speaker stops talking the actors can ad lib their parts.

2. Ask the story teller to go immediately and write a rough outline of the dialogue. This can be done any way they wish: pictures or shorthand — just enough to help them remember. Details can be filled in later if desired.

3. From time to time have the class do group pantomime where they all play the different characters and scenes. Sometimes read

from the book and have them act it out during the reading. The technique of *freezing* and *bring it to life* can be used most effectively.

4. The final job involves selecting the parts. Make a large chart with the names of all the children on it. Another chart can be made with a list of all possible roles, even including minor parts, for group scenes, inanimate objects, prop people and stage crew or assistants. Ask for each child's first and second choice and write their selections next to their name. Also make note of the number of children requesting a particular part.

5. Look the choices over and where there are duplications, have tryouts. A method which works well is to call all those up who are contending for a particular part. First have them pantomime a scene all at once, then call a *freeze* and bring each one to life. If time permits, you can have individual tryouts, but these group tryouts work amazingly well.

6. Make your choice at least in part on the basis of which children are responsible and *considerate,* or even which children might be ready to benefit from a lead role in which they are depended upon by others. *Desire* is a key criteria, because if a child really wants to do something, he'll put his very best efforts into it, and that effort will carry him through.

7. It is helpful to reassure the children that you will try not to take a part away from a child as long as he is willing to work on it, do his *best* and continue to like the role. This is an important factor in helping to create a safe atmosphere. The focus then remains as it should: on the benefits given to the entire class *and* to individual children, rather than excessive worry about a polished performance.

8. If a child doesn't put his best efforts into a part and it becomes apparent you may ask, "Do you still like this part?" or, "Do you *want* to do it?" If their response is hesitant or negative, it can be easily deduced that the *considerate* thing to do is to replace that child and put someone else in who really wants to do it. This can be done with relative ease, because the entire class is familiar with the story, and any child who has the desire to do so can learn a part almost overnight.

9. For the final product, a script need not be used, but a basic outline can serve as a guide when rehearsing. Children need to

be directed not to block one another, to speak out to the audience, and to take turns with their ad libs.

EVALUATION: The student-teacher script is one of the most satisfying experiences of all. This approach is especially exciting when applied to the class study of a work of literature. The children gain a wealth of experience. *Story tellers* eagerly volunteer and skilled script writers emerge. Those who assist, take minor roles or do art work, are every bit as enthusiastic and proud. Their ability to creatively *ad lib* is astonishing; as is their willingness to cooperate with and support one another. The final product is delightful and fresh with a quality about it which is not found in a scripted play. Children are totally involved in their parts, and never lose their enthusiastic energetic delivery. All feel great satisfaction with the results.

TONGUE TWISTERS

GRADES: 3–8

TYPE OF ACTIVITY: Speech exercise involving the entire class, either as solo, group, or game — develops communication skills

GOALS:
1. To help children enunciate more clearly
2. To make a game out of speech
3. To give shy children a chance for success
4. To give confidence to all children

READINESS: Discuss the meaning of the phrase *tongue twister* and talk about how we can get our words mixed up and how some combinations are difficult and confusing. There is a need for clear enunciation. Demonstrate, using some of the samples below.

PROCEDURE:
1. Hand out a sheet to each child and ask that they pick one of the tongue twisters and attempt to memorize it. Give them five minutes to work silently. Have them share, and then give them a partner with whom to work further, if desired.

2. Put them in groups and ask that they think of an entertaining way to present one of the selections.

3. Each child can attempt one, said rapidly, four or five times. Someone can be appointed timekeeper, and someone else keep track of the number of mistakes. One minute can be set as the time, and see how far a child can go down the list, or how many times he can say a particular one (optional).

4. Emphasize the need to stress certain words for meaning, and have them take turns demonstrating their skill at repeating the selection slowly and dramatically.

5. Ask the children to make up one of their own — with optional illustrations.

SPECIAL NEEDS: Children with a speech problem can be allowed much latitude with their selection. Every effort should be made not to embarrass a child.

EVALUATION: This is excellent for pronunciation, and loads of fun. It should be repeated often in a variety of different ways so that *all* the children can benefit from this type of experience and practice.

Tongue Twisters

- Eat fresh fried fish free at the fish fry.
- An old scold sold a cold coal shovel.
- Put a blackbacked bath brush.
- The bootblack brought the black boot back.
- Does your shirt shop stock short socks with spots?
- Each sixth chick sat on a stick.
- Six slim slick sycamore saplings.
- Lilly ladled little Letty's lentil soup.
- Frivolous fat Fanny fried fresh fish furiously on Friday forenoon for four famished families.

Peter Prangle
The prickly prangly pear picker
Picked three packs of prickly prangle pears.

A skunk sat on a stump
The stump thunk the skunk stunk.
The skunk thunk the stump stunk.

My dame hath a lame tame crane.
My dame hath a crane that is lame.
Pray, gentle Jane, let my dame's tame crane
Feed and come home again.

She sells seashells,
So swing sweet singing bells.
Shave a cedar shingle thin,
Let the fun begin.

Theophilus Thistledown,
The successful thistle sifter,
In sifting a sieve of unsifted thistles,
Thrust three thousand thistles
Through the thick of his thumb.

Three crooked cripples went through Cripplegate,
And through Cripplegate went three crooked cripples.

Three grey geese in a green field grazing.
Grey were the geese and green was the grazing.

Swan swam over the sea,
Swim, swan, swim!
Swan swam back again,
Well swum, swan!

When a Twister a-twisting will twist him a twist,
for the twisting of his twist, he three twines doth untwist;
But if one of the twines of the twist do untwist,
The twine that untwisteth, untwisteth the twist.

Billy button bought a buttered biscuit;
A buttered biscuit Billy Button bought.
If Billy Button bought a buttered biscuit,
Where's the buttered biscuit
That billy Button bought?

Sister Susie's sewing socks for soldiers;
Socks for soldiers Sister Susie sews.
If Sister Susie's sewing socks for soldiers,
Where are the socks for soldiers
That Sister Susie sews?

Robert Rowley rolled a round roll round,
A round roll Robert Rowley rolled round;
Where rolled the round roll
Robert Rowley rolled around?

Moses supposes his toeses are roses,
But Moses supposes erroneously;
For nobody's toeses are posies of roses
As Moses supposes his toeses to be.

Peter Piper picked a peck of pickled pepper;
A peck of pickled pepper Peter Piper picked.
If Peter Piper picked a peck of pickled pepper,
Where's the peck of pickled pepper Peter Piper picked?

Some shun sunshine.
Do you shun sunshine?

TRY OUTS
OR AUDITIONS

GRADES: 1–8

TYPE OF ACTIVITY: This lesson helps with the difficult task of selecting parts for a particular production or play.

GOALS:
1. To encourage creative expression.
2. To give individual opportunity for talent to emerge.
3. To provide an activity in which the entire class can participate and benefit from.

MATERIALS: Any appropriate scripts or dialogue ideas.

READINESS: Discuss the meaning of the words "tryout" or "audition." An audition is a hearing to test the suitability for a part of an actor. It is a good idea at this time to discuss disappointment and how one can learn to be a "good sport" is one of the best things you can ever learn to do, as you can *never* get your way about everything, and will be very unhappy if you expect to do so.

PROCEDURE: EXAMPLE A: Divide the group in half. Describe a scene to the acting half, together with feelings and short dialogue, such as: You are very , very excited because you just won the lottery and this is the first time you even tried playing. You look at the winning ticket, become astonished and say, "What? I don't believe it....I've WON....I've WON!"

Demonstrate, then have the entire group do it with you. Next, go one by one down the line and have each actor repeat the same thing alone while the instructor gives nothing but positive comments and even assisting a student when it appears appropriate. Once the first half of the group has finished, call up the second half and repeat.

EXAMPLE B: This activity can be done with the entire class or the group may be divided into watchers and participants. The actors come up and begin acting out in pantomime whatever is being read or said. On the signal FREEZE all freeze. One at a time, either by calling names or lightly touching a student, the actor is instructed to "come to life" with words and actions which they are able to demonstrate. The others should remain frozen until brought to life. Any child who does not wish to "act" at this point, does not have to, nor are they singled out for any possible embarrassment.

EXAMPLE C: Have a list of all possible parts put on the board, or make a ditto and pass it out. Minor and group parts should be listed as well as stage and costume assistants. The teacher gives a brief synopsis of each role and then asks each student to select a first and second choice. When there are several who want the same part, more individualized techniques can be used. (see Example B)

EXAMPLE D: Give out some easy dialogue to be read, first in unison, then as a "copy me" (see index) exercise. Volunteers can be called up to read individually or with several together if there is interaction involved in the scene.

EXAMPLE E: Give the children scripts to take home and study, or give them class time to look them over so they can select their own parts to read or memorize.

EVALUATION: Each example has its special use, but Example A is wonderful for getting *everyone* involved immediately in a non-threatening acting activity.

VERBS

GRADES: 2–8

TYPE OF ACTIVITY: Whole group, pantomime, writing and grammar

MATERIALS: Paper, pencil, or none, if pantomimed

GOALS:
1. To learn about verbs
2. To pantomime, learn through doing
3. To have a creative opportunity for children to think of words of their own.

READINESS: Discuss verbs and how they help create a sentence or thought, only two words being necessary to create a sentence: "I am." "She sits." "He runs." If desired, you may discuss how some verbs are a state of being, some denote action, and some take an object.

PROCEDURE: Do the following appropriately for class level:

1. Use the list for a pantomime activity for the children.

2. Use the list for *Wordo* Game (page 167).

3. Have the children make little drawings illustrating the *verb*.

4. Ask the children to write stories using the words and then act the stories out. Look in magazines for pictures to illustrate the verbs — act out illustrations dramatically if desired.

5. Have them look for which words can be two or more parts of speech such as: verbs, nouns, adjectives, adverbs, eg., *sharp*: a *sharp* in music (noun); a *sharp* knife (adjective); *sharpen* the knife (verb); do it *sharply* (adverb).

   a   act, argue, ask, amble
   b   bawl, break, bandage, brag, beat, burn
   c   chop, cut, clip, cry, call, carry

d draw, drink, dawdle, dip, dunk, drive

e eat, end, edge, elbow

f fall, fit, fumble, fly, force, foretell

g give, glum, glare, glue

h hop, hit, hug, handle (something)

i itch, idolize, idle, increase, inform

j jump, joke, jiggle, juggle

l lick, laugh, loosen, lay, listen, lift, lie

m manage, move, make, mirror, manipulate

n neigh, nudge, nap, note, nod

o order, open, overlook, overtake, oppress, orbit

p push, pull, pitch, pick, play, prance, pat, punch

q quit

r run, reach, rock, roll, ripple

s stretch, skip, sip, switch, swim, ski, spin

t throw, try, turn, tap, twist

w walk, weep, wail, wish, wander, wade

y yell, yodel, yap, yield

SPECIAL NEEDS: Children with special needs will learn much better by *doing*. Their assignment could be to draw a picture or look for pictures, rather than write.

EVALUATION: This is a marvelous way to reinforce the teaching of grammar and stimulate writing. The *doing* by acting reinforces the meaning of the word and is fun.

VOICE WITH AUTHORITY

GRADES: 3–8

TYPE OF ACTIVITY: Curriculum related. Group exercise to promote better oral reading, done in pairs

GOALS:
1. To develop better eye contact
2. To learn to speak with authority
3. To learn to use a clear, strong voice
4. To promote better oral reading and have fun doing it

READINESS: Demonstrate *voice with authority* by saying, *"Five Things Ready"* (page 36). First, in a soft, apologetic voice, and then in a voice that is firm and clear. Naturally, they respond to the voice with the tone of authority. This strong tone and good eye contact is their goal. They are also told to use *only* their voices, no facial or body movements.

PROCEDURE:
1. Children are paired, sitting facing one another, about six inches apart.

2. First they close their eyes and try to concentrate on just *being there*. Have them do this for about one minute.

3. Next they are to open their eyes, look at their partners, and try not to laugh or fidget. This also should be accomplished for a period of about a minute.

4. They are then given books, and one is to be the teacher and the other the student. They take turns with these roles. The student looks at the book, gets a phrase in his mind, looks at his partner, and says the phrase with authority. If the student is not perfect, the teacher says, "Flunk! Do it again!" The teacher also explains just what it was that needs improvement: "You spoke too softly"; "You lifted you eyebrow"; "You bit your lip"; etc.

5. The *teacher* then asks that the same passage be repeated until he (the teacher) can say, "Good!" Each child should get about three "Goods" before switching roles.

6. Partners can be switched also, but when sufficient time (about ten minutes) has been spent, it is well to ask for everyone to be the audience and take volunteers to come up to the front of the room to demonstrate a voice delivered *with authority* and good eye contact.

VARIATION A:	Ask for a volunteer to read aloud to the class using the strengthened voice, and eye contact. It should be emphasized that contact needs to be made with all sides of the room so that no one feels left out.
VARIATION B:	Encourage the reader to try different things: sitting down, standing and moving appropriately, gestures, expression, pauses, and any other device which helps get the meaning of the selection across.
VARIATION C:	Give the children additional practice by asking that they prepare a short reading as a homework assignment. Each child is encouraged to practice looking at a mirror, using gestures, and trying different techniques so they can learn from watching themselves.
EVALUATION:	This is an *excellent* exercise to assist with better oral reading skills. It helps the children to *project their voices* and to *make eye contact*, since most children have insufficient awareness of the importance of these factors in their daily interactions. Oral reading is part of the overall learning process, and encouraging the skill at every opportunity gives a child a feeling of growing security and confidence.

THE W'S OF STORY-MAKING

GRADES: 2–8

TYPE OF ACTIVITY: Small group and individual story writing and acting involving the elements of WHO, WHAT, WHERE, WHY and WHEN

MATERIALS: 3 x 5 inch cards with suggestions for each category

GOALS:
1. To learn the main elements of story making
2. To use creativity and imagination
3. To be involved in simple, beginning group planning
4. To provide a stimulus for writing and acting

READINESS: Discuss what is needed to put a story together, drawing the responses from the students themselves. Just keep asking, "What else would help make the story better?" Emphasize that we want *general* things which would fit for all stories.

PROCEDURE:
1. Once there has been sufficient discussion, put the five terms on the board:

   WHO, WHAT, WHERE, WHY, WHEN

2. Ask for ideas for what to put under each category:

WHO:	doctor, teacher, child
WHAT:	Went for a walk, climbed a mountain
WHERE:	In a park, at school, at home
WHY:	Because he was bored, because they were poor
WHEN:	Last night, a year ago

3. Point to some of the responses listed or call them out and have the class pantomime acting out — any way they wish. do *Audience/Actor* (see page 3).

4. Start putting some items together and have them pantomime acting the scene; i.e., "A child went for a walk in the park at night because he was bored."

5. Use the boxes with the 3 x 5 inch cards and let a child draw one out and act it out, having the class guess.

6. Have someone try drawing out two cards, (one each from different boxes). Try three, four and even five cards.

7. Put the children in groups having the use of the cards optional for ideas and have them act the stories out, first pantomime and then with voice.

8. Ask the children to write their own stories, read aloud, act out.

EVALUATION: This lesson can be used in a great variety of ways but it provides a wonderful stimulus for writing, acting and interacting!

WALK AND TALK

GRADES: 3–8

TYPE OF ACTIVITY: Whole group; active; needs a fairly large space; verbal

GOALS:
1. To promote spontaneous speech
2. To allow an avenue for pent up feelings
3. To demonstrate the usefulness of motion with speaking
4. To help the shy ones to express themselves
5. To provide a good lead-in to speech development

PROCEDURE:
1. It is helpful to have this activity follow a *move around* pantomime exercise such as Emotions, so that the children are already dispersed around the room when calling a *Freeze!*

2. Instruct one of the children to begin *walking and talking. School* is a favorite subject, but anything can be selected: drugs, girls, boys, parents, vacations, teachers, bullies, war, etc., *or* there need be no specific subject selected, but simply request that they put voice to the emotion in which they are frozen.

3. The student is to keep on walking and talking until another child begins, at which point the first child sits down and the second child begins walking and talking.

4. If the class is shy, tap a child, with the understanding that he is to begin talking when tapped. If necessary, keep tapping children until they feel confident enough to carry on on their own.

VARIATION A: Rather than having them sit after speaking, simply have them freeze and let the exercise continue. Those who do not respond can eventually be tapped and told to *say anything!*

VARIATION B: Change the subject with some side coaching — add an ingredient, like, *It's now raining* or *You are lost*...

SPECIAL NEEDS: Children in wheelchairs may participate and need not move (or can be pushed by someone). It is important to include all, assuming they will participate — but never forcing a response.

EVALUATION: This exercise can be repeated often as it has many values: teamwork, speech improvisation, and emotional expression. It is a favorite with all.

WHAT IS IT?

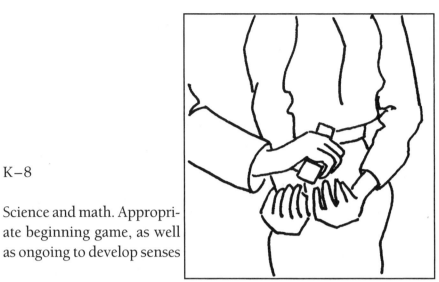

GRADES: K–8

TYPE OF ACTIVITY: Science and math. Appropriate beginning game, as well as ongoing to develop senses

GOALS:
1. To improve concentration on the senses
2. To help children become more aware of shape, size, weight, texture, etc.
3. To expand vocabulary

READINESS: Discuss how we need to use our senses to really learn about things, not to just try to memorize *words*. Talk again about the five senses, but now we are going to focus on the sense of *touch*.

PROCEDURE:
1. A volunteer comes to the front of the class, turns his back and puts his hands behind his back.
2. Ask the class if anyone has anything in their pocket or on their person! Have them hold it up.
3. Make a selection and hold it up for all to see, cautioning the children not to give it away.
4. Put it in the volunteer's hands and ask questions like, "How big is it?, How heavy?, What shape?, What does it feel like?" This continues until the child guesses correctly or gives up.
5. Let the child who contributed the object be the next *guesser*.

VARIATION A: Use geometric shapes, cuissinaire rods, and blocks to teach shapes and sizes.

VARIATION B: Use plants, leaves, flowers or rocks in connection with curriculum studies.

VARIATION C: Make it a homework assignment for children to bring in interesting objects.

VARIATION D: Bring in suitable material to be tasted and smelled, using a blindfold. Have a tray ready and allow the children to examine the articles.

SPECIAL NEEDS: Children with handicaps of any kind benefit from this approach and may be surprisingly *gifted*.

EVALUATION: This game calls for teacher creativity and can be used at all levels to teach any specifics. Using it often and at each grade level reinforces learning and is always fun.

WHO STARTED THE MOTION?

GRADES: K–3

TYPE OF ACTIVITY: Circle game to promote simple skills

GOALS:
1. To sharpen observation skills
2. To promote leadership
3. To promote cooperative feelings and skills

READINESS: This game will involve trying *not* to look at the leader — but rather, to look at someone else in the group to see what motion is being done. This protects the *leader* from discovery. A subtle skill is involved in this game but small children readily pick it up.

PROCEDURE:
1. Have the children form a circle.
2. Ask for a volunteer, and have that child leave the circle and turn his back, reminding him not to *peek*.
3. Choose a *leader*, and caution the group that although they are to copy the leader, they should try not to look directly at the person chosen, but rather to pick up clues from the group as they glance around the circle.
4. The volunteer is called back to stand in the middle of the circle and to try to guess who the leader is.
5. Call out, from time to time, "Change the motion, leader!" Sometimes it helps to suggest that the leader use some facial expressions or dramatic gestures.
6. The guesser can have two chances. If he guesses right, they exchange places. If he can't figure out who it is, the leader stands up and can then choose whether he wants to be *it* or select someone else.

EVALUATION: This game is an excellent ice breaker, or warmer-upper, but can be used at any time as it is always fun and children love it. It is appropriate for drama, as it encourages concentration, cooperation and creativity, as well as good leadership.

WEIRDO

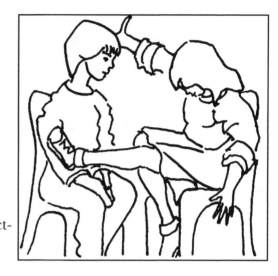

GRADES: 3–8

TYPE OF ACTIVITY: Pairs; group; promotes acting ability.

GOALS:
1. To provide an acting opportunity
2. To have a good time
3. To allow role playing with a chance to play opposite roles

READINESS: Discuss what is meant by *weird* and what our reactions usually are to this kind of behavior, also how sometimes it can be therapeutic and fun to just be *silly*. This exercise will give children an opportunity to be as goofy as they like.

PROCEDURE:
1. Two chairs are set up. Two volunteers are selected.
2. The one on the right is to react honestly to the one on the left or the *Weirdo*. They are cautioned to play it straight.
3. The straight one moves when fed up or when a suitable time frame is over and the *Weirdo* moves into the straight chair and changes roles.
4. This can be done in pairs or with a line so that children wait their turn to go up and play *Weirdo*.

EVALUATION: This is a great release for children. They become very revealing and humorous in their choice of inappropriate actions. The role change is excellent practice for later activities.

WORDO

GRADES: 3–8

TYPE OF ACTIVITY: Vocabulary, grammar, writing and oral reading

GOALS:
1. To expand vocabulary through the use of dramatic words

2. To give children an opportunity to *act out* these words in a non-threatening atmosphere, thereby internalizing their understanding and use of the words

3. To teach grammar by dramatic use of the words selected: verbs, nouns, adjectives, adverbs, etc.

4. To give children experience with direction-taking, involving concentration and observation

5. To involve math terms and concepts: horizontal, vertical, diagonal, $\frac{1}{2}$ of $\frac{1}{2}$, $\frac{1}{4}$ of $\frac{1}{4}$

6. To improve spelling and copying skills

READINESS: Have a discussion on the importance of having a good vocabulary. Not only can you better understand what you're reading, but you can express yourself more effectively and even get better grades. Ask the class for descriptive words and make a list. Point out how the same word can be used as a different part of speech; eg., sharp: noun, play a *sharp*; adjective, a *sharp* knife; verb, *sharpen* the knife; adverb, play *sharply*. This awareness can be used later.

PROCEDURE:
1. Words can be put on the board ahead of time, or a handout made up and distributed. Descriptive words are particularly stimulating. The list should consist of at least twenty to twenty-five words, and can be selected on the basis of coordinating class lessons. It could be a spelling list, a list related to English, social studies, science or math. The teaching of nouns, verbs, adjectives, adverbs, pronouns, prepositions, etc., can subtly be made part of the game.

2. Go over the list quickly, or if preferred, start right out with giving directions. Direction-taking is emphasized as an important skill, requiring their full attention. Remind them that concentration will be one of the most important skills they will need in order to be successful at anything, so they're to get *Five Things Ready* (page 36) as they listen.

Depending on the age and capability of the group, directions are either given all at the same time or may be broken into segments, checking completion before moving on.

3. Tell them to fold the paper in half then in half again, four times, giving sixteen squares (large drawing paper may be used for younger children.) Demonstrate this, and while doing so, discuss the concept of half of a half making a fourth, half of a fourth making an eighth, a fourth of a fourth making a sixteenth.

4. Choosing from the list, instruct them to write one word in each square, except for one, which they leave vacant. This is a FREE square, and they can draw a picture in this space. *Lucky* words can be chosen and written twice (in two squares). They may illustrate the meanings of words if they wish. If it is a class where copying skills need to be emphasized, credit can be given for accurate copying. Those who finish early can draw pictures on the back.

5. It is easy to give the meaning of the words as one goes along with the game by using them in sentences (preferably dramatic ones), and also by acting out the words. It is also very effective to have the class act out the words, eg.:

   • Everyone pantomime being *raucous*;
   • Show that you are *distraught*;
   • Look *ecstatic*;
   • Show that you all are in a state of *euphoria*.

   This enhances their understanding of the words by involving their emotions and physical movements in the learning process.

6. Show them that the game is played like Bingo, and that the object is to get four words in a row (horizontal, vertical or diagonal). Beans or slips of paper can be used to mark the words, but I generally find it more convenient and less messy to have them mark the squares with an *X*, then a check, then underline, then a wavy line, etc. When they do, they are to jump up and shout,

Wordo! The first child to shout *Wordo* is the winner — unless the word is given simultaneously, in which case both win. At this time they can either show or tell what the words mean. This gives them full credit. Credit is given by points. So many points are given to the winner, and a lesser amount given to all participants. Extra points can be given for correct spelling.

Optional Writing Assignment:

Pass out paper and ask them to write. Tell them to use as many *Wordo* words as possible; to underline them and to receive extra credit for the correct use of the words. Encourage a free and flowing style (i.e., to write as if they were talking), and not worry too much about the spelling of words (other than the Wordo words) as long as they can read it. A period of time is specified, usually about five to ten minutes, as this encourages more enthusiastic writing. There is to be no talking or movement during this time, but tell them, "Keep your pencils moving!" This phrase seems to help stimulate the dawdlers.

7. A one minute warning is given to finish up, and then ask for a volunteer or simply call on someone. For the first reading, have them read in whatever manner they wish. Then take the vocabulary words and act them out, exaggerating the motions and including some of the sentences which they have in their writing. It now becomes their turn to try, and hopefully they'll get into the spirit of it and *ham it up*. The class loves it and sees the difference. On the second reading they will generally make eye contact and appropriate significant pauses, and thus get the meaning across. You can ask them to read their work a third time and minimize their acting out of the words, and the improvement in reading skills is phenomenal. A discussion can follow, having to do with what is required for effective oral reading.

EVALUATION: This is an excellent lesson for almost any age or size of group. The dramatization of the words seems to be the essential ingredient to most children for the retention of the meaning. The more involved children get, the more receptive they are to learning; this is why games provide such an excellent means to this end. The body and visual involvement help to internalize their understanding, besides being fun! Children want to do this game again and again, and don't even mind writing. Oral reading skills improve enormously, and shy children overcome their fear of sharing in front of a group.

WRITING AND ACTING IT OUT

GRADES: 2–8

TYPE OF ACTIVITY: Writing and acting, full group

GOALS:
1. To help all key skills: writing, oral expression, and problem solving
2. To provide motivation for writing
3. To involve all children in the process in one way or another
4. To provide an opportunity for original class presentations

READINESS: Talk to children about how writing is often the best when it flows easily, just like you would talk. This is called *organic* writing and is a little different in the sense that we don't worry quite so much about spelling and punctuation just so the writer can read it aloud. Perhaps start to tell a story and have the children volunteer to do the same, thus illustrating that this is the way they are to attempt to write.

PROCEDURE:
1. Give children a theme for writing. They should write at least one page.

   Example A:
   - A terrible day
   - Three wishes
   - When I was surprised
   - Trouble
   - The future, etc.

   Example B:
   Use a list of words emphasizing vocabulary or even grammar (transitive verbs, prepositions, direct objects, etc.) Making this also a drama activity stimulates the children's creativity and enthusiasm. Myths, legends, fables, and adages are especially applicable and effective themes.

Example C:

The following is an excellent list which can be used for all grade levels, as they appeal to children's imagination.

- Why is there thunder?
- Why does the sun sink into the west?
- Why do people walk on two legs instead of four?
- Why does the moon change its shape?
- Why aren't people covered with fur like other animals?
- What causes rain?
- What holds up the earth?
- Why can't men fly like birds?
- What causes the tide?
- What are the stars and how did they get into the sky?
- What causes earthquakes?
- What is the purpose of clouds?
- How did the earth become the home of people?

The children are told that they are perfectly welcome to change anything on the list, or to make up one of their own.

4. Once the stories are written, have them read aloud, using all dramatic expression possible. Try to stress that they are to attempt to hold the attention of the audience, using whatever means they feel appropriate.

5. Select the best to act out.

EVALUATION: This is a favorite activity for any grade level, and one which helps several key skills. Children love the idea of *acting out* their own stories. This motivates them to write. They also are motivated towards leadership roles because they cast and direct their own plays. Older children can be given a theme to write about, and this can be done as homework or *fast writing*, where they are to write as quickly as they can on any theme. This whole activity provides endless possibilities for mini-shows, sharing with other classes or with parents. The fact that the stories are original adds greatly to their value.

APPENDIX

ROLE PLAYING

Third Grade: Problem Situation

Seventh Grade: Drugs and Alcohol

ROLE PLAYING — SAMPLE SCRIPTS

The following rather detailed examples may help give you ideas for a way to start with role plays. Once you feel confident with the procedure, you won't need any script and the children will become increasingly adept and enthusiastic. You will find countless ways to integrate role plays into your curriculum.

Third Grade: Problem Situation

This example is from a third grade classroom. Mrs. Smith had decided to work with the aggression and rivalry which was occurring on the playground and in the neighborhood. Her students were frequently the target of complaint from some of the younger children. It was decided by the class that this was a serious matter which needed attention, and when the teacher suggested role-playing as a possible means of exploring the problem, the idea was greeted favorably.

Mrs. Smith's class had sufficient experience with drama exercises and warm-ups; therefore the problem was approached in the following manner:

> **Mrs. Smith:** I've had a number of complaints about children from this class behaving very unpleasantly to some of the younger children when you're out on the playground. Today I thought we might try acting out a few of these situations that cause problems.
>
> Let's pretend that this area (designates a section of the room) is a very favorite spot on the playground, and some first and second graders are playing a game of Foursquare when some children from third grade come up and demand that they give up this place and go elsewhere. Some of the younger children start to give in, but several others refuse, and unpleasantness occurs. Let's just start with trying to play these roles and see if they look somewhat accurate. Who will volunteer to be first or second graders? (Pauses and looks for hands to be raised) Good. Thank you, Susie, Mary and Jimmy. I saw you raising your hands politely, not begging, so you may play the younger

children for now. The rest of you may also be playing the younger children, so I want you all to watch each part very carefully to see if they play their parts as you think children would actually behave. Now, let's have some volunteers to be third graders. Remember, you have to play a part, and be inconsiderate, which I'm sure will be difficult for most of you, although I guess most all of us have been thoughtless at some time. We do want to learn a better way though, don't we? Thank you, Bobby and Cathy. You may play the third graders who try to bully the younger ones.

(If desired, children may be given different names for the role-playing.)

Let's start the skit. Susie, Mary and Jimmy, you start your imaginary game of Foursquare. Try to work as a team and keep your point of focus on the ball, at least until the argument begins. Mary and Jimmy, you be the ones to give in and Susie, you resist them. You four children in the audience (points) please make special note of how well they bring that imaginary ball to life and work as a team. The rest of you please pay attention to how accurately they portray their roles. Bobby and Cathy, you wait until I signal you, and then go over to the three younger children and be very aggressive.

The actual dialogue of the children is omitted here, as it will vary greatly, but the success of the project is determined by three things: The degree of seriousness and concentration the actors give to their roles; the involvement of the audience as they watch the skit; and the type of discussion which occurs by the entire class in considering the behavior they have just witnessed. Both audience and actors hopefully will suggest several alternative courses of action.

The seriousness and concentration on the part of both the actors and the audience is an essential ingredient which should be part of the goal. There may be laughter, some appropriate and some inappropriate, and it is a delicate balance for the teacher to maintain a safe atmosphere for experimentation and still point out that inappropriate behavior which is destructive. I use comments such as:

"Is it being considerate to Bobby to laugh so hard when he really is trying to play a role? Let's remember feelings."

"Who kept their character especially well and didn't laugh but made you feel their feelings?"

It should be pointed out that there need not be a solution to the problem, nor does the teacher need to sermonize. The awareness and discussion which will ensue from this type of role play will almost certainly help to better the situation. There may be classes where the chemistry is such that this exercise is not as successful as others. It is up to the teacher not to get drawn into the negativity, but to attempt to find a solution.

Further evaluation might have to do with what has been learned by this activity: how it feels to be bullied; what type of children do the bullying and why; how they can best be helped; what is meant by a compromise. These discussions should be spontaneous enough so that the class does not get restless and bored. The teacher should constantly be aware during these role-playing activities of the tone of the class, and try to keep the action and energy going. The actors themselves can switch roles as this gives them an opportunity to feel the opposite emotions and then new volunteers can be picked for the same role play.

Some children may suggest other similar situations; in fact, they usually do. Some representative subjects are:

- Sometimes someone steals a ball;
- Lots of kids won't include younger ones in a game;
- I've heard someone making fun of a new kid;
- Girls are treated mean by boys;

The teacher can suggest some of her own, elaborate on a particular suggestion or stick to the original roleplay and keep making subtle changes.

Seventh Grade: Drugs & Alcohol

This example is a seventh grade class. Mrs. Adams is the teacher, and it has come to her attention that there is a recurring problem with drugs and alcohol. The class is well aware of this, and has had ample drug education, but most are still reluctant to bring their feelings out in the open. There are many aspects of the problem which even the teacher does not understand.

Mrs. Adams: Class, I'd like to do some role-playing with you today. If you recall, role-playing is attempting to play someone else as they would behave in real life in a true-to-life situation. The situation I would like to have you address is that concerning young people with drugs and alcohol. Later I will put you into groups and you will plan your own skits, but first I will help you set one up and the rest of us will be a very observant audience. For this one, I'm going to give you different names and characters, because I want you to try to play someone entirely different from yourselves.

The first character is Mary, a sixth grader, new to the school, very shy and eager to be liked. Who will volunteer to play Mary? (Selects from volunteers.)

The next role is rather difficult, because it's unlike any of you, I'm sure, but we'll need someone to try to talk Mary into trying out some drugs. This person is a successful student and a salesman type. (Selects a boy or girl and gives them a name. Avoid using names of actual children in class. This exercise can also be done without using names at all.)

Now let's have several other children involved in this scene: a friend for Mary and a friend for our pusher. (Selects and cautions them to be support actors.)

Now for a location and time. Let's say it's before school and at some isolated spot on the school yard. Maybe over by that big clump of trees at the back. That's the basic plot, but you may develop it any way you wish once you get the feel of the character.

Mrs. Adams then allowed the action to begin. It was necessary in this case to remind the actors to share with the audience and not do it just for themselves. Reminders were also given to have one person only talk at a time, but at the same time Mrs. Adams was careful not to choke off the spontaneity of the role-play. The comments from the audience should be non-judgmental and supportive, especially to start with, because it is essential that a safe atmosphere be maintained, as this is a personal and delicate area in their real lives, and may touch off some volatile feelings. It's a good idea to vary this scene several times before going on. The teacher took suggestions from the class and was not critical. The next step was to put the children in groups and instruct them to come up with their own dramas having to do with the problem and trying to keep them as true-to-life as possible. The discussions were of great value in bringing things out in the open, allowing discussion as to alternate possible solutions, and an evaluation of morals and ethics without the pontification which sometimes occur in adult lectures. There was a remarkable lifting of feelings after these role-plays; a relief, almost as though there had been a class confession. All too often feelings that are critical are kept hidden and can do damage. That is why role-plays, properly handled, can do much towards improving the tone of a class, as well as giving another dimension to any young person who is attempting to sort out personal problems.

BIBLIOGRAPHY ROLE PLAYING:

Kay, L., and J. Schick, "Role Playing as a Teaching Aid," *Sociometry*, 1949. Aid in teaching, inter-group psychology.

Klein, A.F., "How to Use Role Playing Effectively," *NY Associated Press,* 1959. Useful for leading role playing sessions.

Shaftel, G., "Role Playing and the Problem Story." *NY National Conference of Christians and Jews,* 1952. Emphasis on human relationships.